ROBERTO MIGUEL RODRIGUEZ

Latin America's Political, Social, and Economic Changes in the Last Half Century

Copyright Page

TITLE: Latin America's Political, Social, and Economic Changes in the Last Half Century

1ST Edition

Copyright @ 2023

ISBN: 9798223441267

Table of Contents

Latin America's Political, Social, and Economic Changes in the Last Half Century

By Roberto Miguel Rodriguez

Introduction:

Dedicated to diplomats and politicians who seek to understand Latin America's journey towards progress, this book explores the dynamic landscape of the region. While the suggested outline serves as a guide, it is important to note that the content and organization of the chapters may vary based on the author's preferences and research.

The Political, Social and Economic Changes of Latin America During the Last Half Century

This chapter sets the stage for the subsequent discussions by providing an overview of the key political, social, and economic transformations that have shaped Latin America in the last fifty years. It delves into the historical context, examining the region's challenges, achievements, and aspirations.

The Impact of Neoliberal Economic Policies on Latin American Economies

Here, we analyze the influence of neoliberal economic policies on Latin American economies. Through case studies and empirical evidence, we explore the successes, failures, and unintended consequences of these policies, shedding light on the complex relationship between economic reforms and societal development.

Political Transitions and Democratization Processes in Latin America

This chapter focuses on the political transitions and democratization processes that have taken place in Latin America. It examines the challenges faced during the shift from authoritarian regimes to democratic systems, highlighting the role of key actors and institutions in shaping the region's political landscape.

Social Movements and their Role in Shaping Latin American Societies

Latin America has witnessed numerous social movements that have played a crucial role in shaping societies. This chapter explores the origins, goals, and impacts of these movements, emphasizing their contribution to social change, equity, and justice.

The Rise of Populism in Latin America

Examining the rise of populism, this chapter analyzes its causes, manifestations, and consequences in Latin America. By examining specific cases, we aim to provide a comprehensive understanding of the political, economic, and social implications of populism in the region.

The Effects of Foreign Intervention on Latin American Politics and Economies

This chapter delves into the effects of foreign intervention on Latin American politics and economies. It examines the historical and contemporary impact of external influences, discussing issues such as imperialism, foreign aid, trade agreements, and geopolitical interests.

Indigenous Rights and their Recognition in Latin American Countries

Highlighting the struggles and achievements of indigenous communities, this chapter explores the recognition and protection of indigenous rights in Latin American countries. It delves into the challenges faced by these communities and the ongoing efforts to promote inclusion, cultural preservation, and empowerment.

Gender Equality and Women's Empowerment in Latin America

Focusing on gender equality and women's empowerment, this chapter examines the progress made and the persistent challenges faced by women in Latin America. It explores the role of legislation, social movements, and cultural shifts in promoting gender equity and dismantling gender-based discrimination.

Environmental Challenges and Sustainability in Latin America

This chapter sheds light on the environmental challenges and sustainability issues faced by Latin America. It examines the region's rich biodiversity, natural resources, and the efforts made to balance economic development with environmental preservation.

The Role of International Organizations in Shaping Latin American Policies

Analyzing the role of international organizations, this chapter explores how institutions such as the United Nations, World Bank, and Inter-American Development Bank have influenced Latin American policies. It examines the dynamics of cooperation, advocacy, and the challenges faced by these organizations in addressing regional issues.

The Influence of Globalization on Latin American Economies and Cultures

The final chapter delves into the influence of globalization on Latin American economies and cultures. It analyzes the impact of trade, migration, and technological advancements, discussing the opportunities and challenges posed by globalization for the region.

Conclusion:

This book serves as a comprehensive exploration of Latin America's path to progress, focusing on the political, social, and economic changes that have shaped the region in the last half-century. By examining various topics, it aims to provide diplomats and politicians with a nuanced understanding of Latin America's complexities, challenges, and potential for future growth and development.

Chapter 1: The Political, Social, and Economic Changes of Latin America During the Last Half Century

Political Changes in Latin America

Latin America has witnessed significant political changes over the last half century, transforming the region's political landscape and shaping its societies. This subchapter explores the various political transitions, democratization processes, and the rise of populism in Latin America, offering insights into the impact of these changes on the region's social and economic development.

One of the key aspects covered in this subchapter is the political transitions and democratization processes in Latin America. The region has experienced a shift from authoritarian regimes to democratic governments, with many countries adopting democratic systems and holding regular elections. This transition has been instrumental in fostering political stability, ensuring the protection of human rights, and promoting social and economic progress.

Moreover, the rise of populism in Latin America has had a profound impact on the region's political dynamics. Populist leaders have emerged, appealing to the marginalized and promising radical changes to address social inequalities. However, the effects of populism on governance and economic stability have been varied, with some countries experiencing positive transformations while others facing challenges and setbacks.

Foreign intervention has also played a significant role in shaping Latin American politics and economies. External influences, both positive and negative, have affected the region's political stability and economic development. This subchapter examines the effects of foreign intervention, highlighting instances of intervention that have either supported or hindered progress in the region.

Furthermore, the recognition and protection of indigenous rights in Latin American countries have gained prominence in recent years. This subchapter delves into the struggles faced by indigenous communities and the steps taken by governments to acknowledge their rights and promote their inclusion in political processes.

Gender equality and women's empowerment have also come to the forefront of political discussions in Latin America. The subchapter explores the progress made in this area, highlighting the challenges that women continue to face and the policies implemented to promote gender equality in the region.

Lastly, the subchapter addresses the environmental challenges and sustainability in Latin America. The region is home to diverse ecosystems and natural resources, and the subchapter delves into the efforts made by governments and civil society to address environmental issues and promote sustainable development.

In conclusion, this subchapter provides a comprehensive analysis of the political changes in Latin America over the last half century. It examines the impact of these changes on social and economic development, exploring the role of political transitions, populism, foreign intervention, indigenous rights, gender equality, and environmental challenges. Diplomats and politicians will find this subchapter invaluable in understanding the complex dynamics and opportunities for progress in the region. Moreover, it offers insights into the role of international organizations and the influence of globalization on Latin American policies.

Decolonization and the emergence of independent nations

Introduction:

Decolonization is a significant chapter in Latin America's history, marking the region's journey towards political, social, and economic independence. This subchapter explores the impact of decolonization on Latin American nations and their subsequent emergence as independent entities. It delves into the political, social, and economic changes that shaped the region during the last half century, addressing the audience of diplomats and politicians.

Political Transitions and Democratization Processes:

The decolonization process in Latin America was accompanied by political transitions and the emergence of democratic systems. This subchapter analyzes the democratization processes in various countries, highlighting the challenges and achievements in establishing stable governments and institutions. It explores the role of political parties, civil society, and international organizations in promoting democratic values and ensuring a smooth transition from colonial rule.

Social Movements and Their Role in Shaping Latin American Societies:

Social movements have played a crucial role in shaping Latin American societies during decolonization. This section examines the impact of social movements such as labor unions, student movements, and indigenous rights movements. It analyzes their demands for social justice, equality, and recognition, and how these movements have influenced policy-making and societal transformations.

The Rise of Populism in Latin America:

Populism has been a recurring phenomenon in Latin America, often emerging as a response to political and economic challenges. This subchapter explores the rise of populist leaders and their impact on the region's governance and policies. It examines the factors that contribute to the popularity of populist movements and the consequences of their rule on democratic institutions and social cohesion.

The Effects of Foreign Intervention on Latin American Politics and Economies:

Foreign intervention has historically influenced Latin American politics and economies. This section analyzes the impact of foreign powers on the region's internal affairs, including economic policies, political alliances, and conflicts. It examines the consequences of these interventions on Latin American nations, their sovereignty, and their efforts towards self-determination.

Indigenous Rights and Their Recognition in Latin American Countries:

Decolonization has led to a growing recognition of indigenous rights in Latin American countries. This subchapter explores the progress made in acknowledging and protecting the rights of indigenous populations. It discusses the challenges faced by indigenous communities and the efforts made to promote their cultural heritage, land rights, and political representation.

Conclusion:

Decolonization has been a transformative process for Latin America, leading to the emergence of independent nations and significant political, social, and economic changes. This subchapter highlights the importance of understanding the impact of decolonization on the region's political transitions, social movements, and economic policies. It underscores the need for diplomats and politicians to recognize the challenges and achievements in Latin America's path towards progress, and to work towards fostering sustainable development, social justice, and democratic governance in the region.

Military dictatorships and their impact on political stability

Military dictatorships have played a significant role in shaping the political stability of Latin American countries over the last half century. These authoritarian regimes, often characterized by the centralization of power in the hands of a military leader, have had both positive and negative impacts on the region's political landscape.

On one hand, military dictatorships have been associated with periods of relative stability and order. By imposing strict control over the population and suppressing dissent, these regimes have managed to maintain a semblance of political stability in countries plagued by political turmoil and social unrest. This has been particularly evident during times of economic crisis or social upheaval, when military leaders have stepped in to restore order and prevent the collapse of the state.

However, the stability provided by military dictatorships often comes at the expense of civil liberties and democratic principles. These regimes have a notorious track record of human rights abuses, including torture, disappearances, and extrajudicial killings. The suppression of political opposition and the restriction of civil liberties have stifled democratic processes and hindered the development of a vibrant and inclusive political system.

Moreover, the economic impact of military dictatorships has been mixed. While some regimes have implemented policies that promote economic growth and development, others have pursued short-term gains at the expense of long-term stability. The lack of transparency and accountability in decision-making processes has often resulted in corruption and mismanagement of public resources, undermining the potential for sustainable economic development.

The impact of military dictatorships on political stability in Latin America has not been uniform. Some countries, such as Chile under Augusto Pinochet, have managed to transition to democracy relatively smoothly, with the military gradually returning to the barracks and civilian governments taking over. In other cases, such as Argentina under the military junta, the transition to democracy has been marked by violence and instability.

In conclusion, military dictatorships have had a significant impact on political stability in Latin America over the last half century. While these regimes have at times provided a sense of order and stability, they have also suppressed democratic processes and violated human rights. The long-term effects of military rule on the region's political, social, and economic development continue to be felt today. It is crucial for diplomats and politicians to understand this complex history in order to effectively address the challenges and opportunities facing Latin America in the 21st century.

Transition to democratic governments

Over the last half century, Latin America has witnessed significant political, social, and economic changes. One of the most remarkable transformations has been the transition to democratic governments across the region. This subchapter aims to explore the processes and challenges involved in this transition, shedding light on the experiences of Latin American countries.

The transition to democracy in Latin America has been a complex and multifaceted journey. Many countries in the region were under authoritarian rule, characterized by military dictatorships or oligarchic regimes. However, starting in the 1980s, a wave of democratization swept across the continent, leading to the establishment of democratic governments in most countries.

The impact of neoliberal economic policies on Latin American economies played a crucial role in shaping the transition to democracy. These policies, which emphasized free markets, privatization, and deregulation, were often implemented in conjunction with political liberalization. The combination of economic and political reforms paved the way for democratic transitions, as they created opportunities for civil society organizations, political parties, and social movements to demand greater political participation and accountability.

Political transitions and democratization processes in Latin America were not without challenges. Many countries faced institutional weaknesses, corruption, and inequality, hindering the consolidation of democratic systems. Additionally, social movements played a vital role in shaping Latin American societies during this period, advocating for human rights, indigenous rights, gender equality, and environmental sustainability.

The rise of populism in Latin America has also influenced the transition to democratic governments. Populist leaders often capitalized on social grievances and dissatisfaction with the establishment, promising radical changes and challenging traditional political elites. While populism has had both positive and negative effects, it has contributed to the diversification of political landscapes in the region.

Foreign intervention has had a significant impact on Latin American politics and economies. Historical interventions by global powers have shaped the region's political dynamics, often undermining democratic processes. However, international organizations have also played a crucial role in shaping Latin American policies, promoting democratic governance, human rights, and sustainable development.

Recognizing indigenous rights and achieving gender equality have been important milestones in Latin America's path towards progress.

Indigenous communities have fought for their recognition and participation in decision-making processes, challenging historical marginalization. Similarly, women's empowerment and gender equality have gained momentum, leading to greater representation and opportunities for women in politics and society.

Environmental challenges and sustainability have become pressing issues in Latin America. The region's rich biodiversity and natural resources are under threat due to unsustainable practices. Governments and civil society organizations have increasingly focused on promoting sustainable development and addressing climate change, recognizing the importance of environmental stewardship for future generations.

In conclusion, the transition to democratic governments in Latin America has been a transformative process, driven by a combination of economic reforms, social movements, and political changes. While challenges persist, the region has made significant strides towards democratic governance, indigenous rights, gender equality, and environmental sustainability. The role of international organizations, the impact of globalization, and the effects of foreign intervention have all shaped Latin American policies and influenced the ongoing journey towards progress.

Challenges in establishing strong political institutions

In the last half century, Latin America has witnessed significant political, social, and economic changes. However, the establishment of strong political institutions continues to pose challenges for the region. This subchapter aims to shed light on the obstacles that diplomats and politicians face in their efforts to build robust political institutions in Latin America.

One of the primary challenges lies in the impact of neoliberal economic policies on Latin American economies. These policies, which prioritize free markets and limited state intervention, have often resulted in unequal distribution of wealth, exacerbating social and economic disparities in the region. As a result, political institutions are confronted with the task of addressing these inequalities and creating inclusive policies that benefit all segments of society.

Furthermore, political transitions and democratization processes in Latin America have been marred by instability and polarization. The transition from authoritarian regimes to democracies has been accompanied by power struggles, corruption, and weak institutions. Establishing a solid democratic foundation requires not only free and fair elections but also the strengthening of political parties, rule of law, and accountability mechanisms.

Social movements have played a crucial role in shaping Latin American societies, often demanding greater social justice and political participation. However, their influence also presents challenges for political institutions, as they can disrupt the status quo and complicate decision-making processes. Balancing the demands of social movements with the need for stable governance is a delicate task for policymakers.

Another challenge is the rise of populism in Latin America, which has seen charismatic leaders gain support by appealing to the frustrations and grievances of marginalized populations. While populism can be a catalyst for change, it also poses risks to democratic institutions, as it often concentrates power in the hands of a single leader and undermines checks and balances.

Foreign intervention has historically had a significant impact on Latin American politics and economies. External actors have often pursued their own interests, leading to political instability and economic dependency. Overcoming these challenges requires strengthening national sovereignty and fostering regional cooperation to reduce external interference.

Additionally, recognizing and protecting the rights of indigenous communities remains a challenge for political institutions. Indigenous peoples have long been marginalized and face discrimination in various aspects of their lives. Ensuring their inclusion and participation in political processes is essential for building inclusive societies.

Gender equality and women's empowerment also demand attention from political institutions. Despite progress in some areas, Latin America still faces gender disparities in political representation, economic opportunities, and access to education and healthcare. Political institutions must prioritize policies that promote gender equality and empower women to participate fully in decision-making processes.

Environmental challenges and sustainability are pressing issues in Latin America. Political institutions must address deforestation, pollution, and climate change, while balancing economic development with environmental conservation.

The role of international organizations in shaping Latin American policies cannot be ignored. Institutions such as the United Nations and the Organization of American States play a crucial role in promoting democracy, human rights, and sustainable development in the region.

Lastly, the influence of globalization on Latin American economies and cultures presents both opportunities and challenges. Political institutions must navigate the complexities of global trade, investment, and cultural exchange while preserving national identity and sovereignty.

In conclusion, establishing strong political institutions in Latin America is a multifaceted challenge. Overcoming the obstacles outlined in this subchapter requires policymakers to address socioeconomic disparities, strengthen democracy, engage with social movements, mitigate the risks of populism and foreign intervention, protect the rights of indigenous communities and women, ensure environmental sustainability, and navigate the complexities of globalization. By tackling these challenges head-on, Latin America can pave its path to progress and build a more inclusive and prosperous future.

Social Changes in Latin America

Latin America has witnessed significant social changes over the last half century, which have shaped the region's political, social, and economic landscape. These changes have been driven by various factors, including the impact of neoliberal economic policies, political transitions, social movements, foreign intervention, indigenous rights, gender equality, environmental challenges, and the influence of globalization.

One of the key aspects of social change in Latin America has been the impact of neoliberal economic policies on the region's economies. These policies, which emphasize free markets and limited government intervention, have had mixed results. While they have led to economic growth and increased foreign investment in some countries, they have also exacerbated income inequality and marginalized certain sectors of society. It is crucial for diplomats and politicians to understand the nuances of these policies and their effects on Latin American economies.

Political transitions and democratization processes have also played a significant role in shaping Latin America. Many countries in the region have transitioned from authoritarian regimes to more democratic systems, allowing for greater political participation and representation. However, challenges related to corruption, weak institutions, and the consolidation of power remain, and efforts to strengthen democracy in the region should be a priority for policymakers.

The rise of social movements in Latin America has been instrumental in advocating for change and shaping societies. From indigenous rights movements to women's empowerment and environmental activism, these movements have brought attention to key issues and pushed for policy reforms. Diplomats and politicians must recognize the role of social movements in driving social change and work towards inclusive and participatory governance.

Additionally, the rise of populism in Latin America has had a profound impact on the region's politics and societies. Populist leaders have gained popularity by tapping into the frustrations and grievances of marginalized groups, but their policies and rhetoric have often been divisive and polarizing. Understanding the causes and consequences of populism is crucial for diplomats and politicians seeking to address the challenges faced by Latin America.

Foreign intervention has also played a significant role in shaping Latin American politics and economies. Historical interventions, both overt and covert, have often had negative consequences for the region, including political instability, economic dependency, and social unrest. It is essential for diplomats and politicians to consider the effects of foreign intervention and work towards mutually beneficial relationships.

Recognition of indigenous rights and gender equality are fundamental components of social change in Latin America. Efforts to respect and protect indigenous rights and empower women have gained momentum, leading to greater inclusion and representation. Policymakers must continue supporting these efforts and ensure that indigenous communities and women have equal access to opportunities and resources.

Environmental challenges and sustainability are pressing issues in Latin America. Deforestation, pollution, and climate change pose significant threats to the region's natural resources and communities. Diplomats and politicians must prioritize environmental protection and work towards sustainable development models that balance economic growth with environmental conservation.

Finally, international organizations play a crucial role in shaping Latin American policies. Organizations such as the United Nations, World Bank, and International Monetary Fund provide financial and technical assistance, but their policies and conditionality measures must align with the region's needs and priorities. Diplomats and politicians should actively engage with these organizations to ensure that their policies are inclusive, equitable, and responsive to the region's challenges.

In conclusion, social changes in Latin America have been driven by various factors and have had a profound impact on the region's political, social, and economic landscape. Understanding these changes is crucial for diplomats and politicians to effectively address the challenges and opportunities that lie ahead. By recognizing the complexity of social changes in Latin America, policymakers can work towards promoting inclusive, sustainable, and equitable development in the region.

Urbanization and its effects on society

Urbanization refers to the process of population migration from rural areas to urban centers, resulting in the growth and expansion of cities. In the context of Latin America, urbanization has had profound effects on society, shaping the political, social, and economic landscape of the region over the last half-century.

One of the key impacts of urbanization in Latin America has been the transformation of traditional rural societies into modern urban ones. As people flock to cities in search of better economic opportunities, the social fabric of communities changes. This shift has led to the emergence of new social movements, such as labor unions and grassroots organizations, which have played a crucial role in advocating for the rights of marginalized groups and shaping public policies.

Moreover, urbanization has brought about significant political transitions and democratization processes in Latin America. As cities become the epicenter of power and influence, politicians and diplomats have had to adapt to the changing dynamics of urban societies. The rise of urban populations has led to the rise of populism in the region, with charismatic leaders capitalizing on the discontent and demands of urban dwellers.

The effects of foreign intervention on Latin American politics and economies have also been magnified by urbanization. As cities become hubs of economic activity and investment, they become more susceptible to the influence of foreign powers and multinational corporations. This has both positive and negative consequences, as foreign intervention can bring economic growth and development, but also exacerbate social inequalities and environmental challenges.

Additionally, urbanization has had a significant impact on gender equality and women's empowerment in Latin America. As women increasingly move to cities, they gain access to education, job opportunities, and reproductive health services. However, they also face unique challenges such as gender-based violence and discrimination, which require targeted policies and social movements to address.

Furthermore, the environmental challenges and sustainability in Latin America are closely tied to urbanization. Rapid urban growth often leads to increased pollution, deforestation, and resource depletion, posing significant threats to the region's ecosystems and biodiversity. Policymakers and international organizations have a crucial role to play in promoting sustainable urban planning and development.

In conclusion, urbanization has been a catalyst for political, social, and economic changes in Latin America over the last half-century. Diplomats and politicians need to understand the multifaceted effects of urbanization in order to address the challenges and opportunities it presents. By recognizing the role of social movements, promoting gender equality, addressing environmental challenges, and navigating the influence of foreign powers, policymakers can shape a more inclusive, sustainable, and prosperous future for Latin America.

Inequality and social stratification

In the last half century, Latin America has experienced significant political, social, and economic changes that have shaped the region's development. One crucial aspect that cannot be overlooked is the persistent issue of inequality and social stratification. This subchapter aims to shed light on the challenges posed by these issues and their impact on Latin American societies.

Latin America has long been plagued by deep-rooted inequality, with a small elite controlling a disproportionate share of wealth and power. This has resulted in stark social stratification, where individuals are divided into distinct social classes based on their economic status. The consequences of this divide are far-reaching, affecting access to education, healthcare, and even basic necessities for the most vulnerable populations.

The impact of neoliberal economic policies on Latin American economies has further exacerbated inequality and social stratification. These policies, which promote free markets and limited government intervention, have often led to the concentration of wealth in the hands of a few, while the majority struggle to make ends meet. As a result, the gap between the rich and the poor has widened, leading to increased social unrest and political instability.

Political transitions and democratization processes in Latin America have played a significant role in addressing inequality and social stratification. The region has witnessed the rise of social movements advocating for more inclusive societies and equal opportunities for all. Grassroots organizations have mobilized to demand better living conditions, land rights, and social justice. These movements have played a crucial role in shaping Latin American societies and pushing for policies that address inequality.

The rise of populism in Latin America has also been closely linked to the issue of inequality. Populist leaders have capitalized on the discontent caused by social stratification and have promised to address the needs of the marginalized populations. However, their policies have often been polarizing and have not always yielded sustainable solutions to inequality.

Foreign intervention has had a profound impact on Latin American politics and economies, often exacerbating inequality. Historically, external powers have influenced the region's policies and resource exploitation, further deepening social divisions. It is crucial for diplomats and politicians to recognize the negative effects of foreign intervention and work towards more equitable partnerships that promote sustainable development.

In recent years, there has been a growing recognition of indigenous rights and the need for their inclusion in Latin American countries. Indigenous communities have long been marginalized and their rights violated. Efforts are now being made to acknowledge their cultural heritage, land rights, and political representation, aiming to reduce inequality and promote social cohesion.

Gender equality and women's empowerment have also gained momentum in Latin America. Women's rights movements have fought for equal opportunities, access to education, and an end to gender-based violence. Policies promoting gender equality and women's empowerment have been implemented, but there is still much work to be done to bridge the gender gap and ensure equal rights for all.

Environmental challenges and sustainability in Latin America have also been closely linked to inequality. Indigenous communities and marginalized populations are often disproportionately affected by environmental degradation and climate change. Diplomats and politicians must address these challenges through sustainable policies that promote social equity and protect the environment for future generations.

International organizations play a crucial role in shaping Latin American policies and addressing inequality. They provide financial support, technical expertise, and advocacy for social and economic reforms. Collaborating with these organizations can help create a more inclusive and equitable society in Latin America.

Lastly, globalization has had a profound impact on Latin American economies and cultures. While it has brought economic opportunities, it has also increased inequality and social divisions. Diplomats and politicians must navigate the challenges of globalization to ensure that its benefits are shared equitably and that local cultures and identities are preserved.

In conclusion, addressing inequality and social stratification is crucial for the political, social, and economic progress of Latin America.

Diplomats and politicians must prioritize policies that reduce inequality, promote social mobility, and ensure equal opportunities for all. By working towards a more inclusive and equitable society, Latin America can overcome the challenges it faces and achieve sustainable development.

Poverty reduction and social welfare programs

Poverty reduction and social welfare programs have been crucial in shaping Latin America's path to progress over the last half century. These initiatives have played a significant role in addressing the region's economic and social challenges, improving the lives of millions of people, and fostering a more equitable society.

Latin America has long been plagued by high levels of poverty and income inequality. However, in recent decades, governments across the region have implemented a range of poverty reduction programs aimed at improving living conditions and providing basic social services to the most vulnerable populations. These programs have included conditional cash transfer programs, access to education and healthcare, and job creation initiatives.

One of the most successful poverty reduction programs in Latin America is Brazil's Bolsa Família. This program provides cash transfers to low-income families, conditional on their children attending school and receiving regular healthcare check-ups. Bolsa Família has lifted millions of Brazilians out of poverty and has been recognized as a model for other countries in the region.

While social welfare programs have made significant strides in reducing poverty, they have also faced challenges. Limited resources, corruption, and political instability have sometimes hindered the effectiveness and sustainability of these programs. Additionally, the region's high levels of informality and inequality have posed obstacles to reaching the most marginalized populations.

In recent years, there has been a growing recognition of the need for a comprehensive approach to poverty reduction that addresses not only income poverty but also other dimensions of deprivation, such as access to education, healthcare, and adequate housing. This shift towards a more holistic approach reflects a broader understanding of poverty as a multidimensional issue that requires targeted interventions.

Furthermore, social welfare programs have also served as a tool for social inclusion and addressing historical inequalities. Efforts have been made to ensure that these programs reach marginalized groups, such as indigenous communities and Afro-Latinos, who have historically faced discrimination and exclusion. Recognition of indigenous rights and gender equality have also been important components of poverty reduction strategies in the region.

Overall, poverty reduction and social welfare programs have played a critical role in Latin America's path to progress. By addressing the root causes of poverty and inequality, these initiatives have not only improved the lives of millions but also contributed to a more inclusive and equitable society. However, ongoing efforts are needed to strengthen these programs, ensure their sustainability, and address the remaining challenges of poverty and social exclusion in the region.

Education and healthcare reforms

Education and healthcare reforms have played a crucial role in the political, social, and economic changes that Latin America has undergone in the last half century. These reforms have been instrumental in addressing the region's challenges and promoting progress in various fields.

In terms of education, Latin America has made significant strides in improving access and quality. Governments have recognized the importance of education in reducing poverty, inequality, and promoting social mobility. As a result, there have been efforts to increase enrollment rates, improve infrastructure, and enhance teacher training. Additionally, policies have focused on expanding access to higher education and technical training to meet the demands of a changing job market.

Healthcare reforms have also been a priority in Latin America. Governments have recognized the need to provide affordable and accessible healthcare to all citizens. Efforts have been made to expand coverage, improve healthcare infrastructure, and enhance the quality of services. These reforms have been crucial in reducing infant mortality rates, increasing life expectancy, and addressing prevalent diseases such as HIV/AIDS and malaria.

Education and healthcare reforms have not only improved the well-being of individuals but have also had significant economic impacts. A well-educated and healthy population is essential for economic growth and development. It enables individuals to acquire skills, participate in the labor market, and contribute to the overall productivity of the country. Moreover, investments in education and healthcare can lead to innovation, research, and development, which are vital for long-term economic competitiveness.

However, challenges remain in the implementation and sustainability of these reforms. Limited resources, inadequate infrastructure, and unequal access to quality education and healthcare persist in many Latin American countries. Additionally, political and social factors, such as corruption, social inequality, and cultural barriers, can hinder the effectiveness of these reforms.

To address these challenges, it is crucial for diplomats and politicians to prioritize education and healthcare reforms in their policy agendas. International cooperation and support can play a vital role in providing funding, technical assistance, and knowledge sharing. Furthermore, it is essential to involve all stakeholders, including local communities, civil society organizations, and international organizations, in the decision-making processes to ensure that reforms are inclusive and address the specific needs of different populations.

In conclusion, education and healthcare reforms have been pivotal in reshaping Latin America over the last half century. These reforms have contributed to reducing inequality, promoting social mobility, and fostering economic development. However, further efforts are needed to overcome the remaining challenges and ensure that all citizens have access to quality education and healthcare services. By prioritizing these reforms, diplomats and politicians can contribute to the progress and well-being of Latin American societies.

Economic Changes in Latin America

Over the past half century, Latin America has experienced significant economic transformations that have shaped the region's development and trajectory. This subchapter explores the economic changes in Latin America and their implications on the political and social landscape of the region.

Latin America's economic journey during the last 50 years has been marked by a shift from state-led development strategies to neoliberal economic policies. The impact of these policies on Latin American economies has been both transformative and controversial. The adoption of market-oriented reforms, such as privatization, trade liberalization, and deregulation, aimed to promote economic growth and attract foreign investments. While some argue that these policies have contributed to economic progress and integration into the global market, others criticize their negative effects on income distribution and social equity.

Political transitions and democratization processes have also played a crucial role in shaping the economic landscape of Latin America. As countries transitioned from authoritarian regimes to democratic governments, economic policies became subject to public scrutiny and debate. Governments had to balance the demands of social movements and popular pressure for greater equality and inclusion with the need to attract foreign investments and promote economic stability.

The rise of populism in Latin America has also had significant economic implications. Populist leaders often championed redistributive policies and social welfare programs, seeking to address historical inequalities. However, these policies were not always sustainable and sometimes led to economic instability and fiscal challenges.

Foreign intervention has had a profound impact on Latin American politics and economies. Historical interventions by major world powers have influenced the region's economic policies, often prioritizing their own geopolitical interests over local development needs. This has led to tensions and conflicts, as Latin American countries seek to assert their sovereignty and pursue their own economic agenda.

Additionally, the subchapter examines other key topics relevant to diplomats and politicians in Latin America. It explores indigenous rights and their recognition in Latin American countries, gender equality, women's empowerment, environmental challenges, and sustainability. It also delves into the role of international organizations in shaping Latin American policies and the influence of globalization on the region's economies and cultures.

Understanding the economic changes in Latin America is essential for diplomats and politicians as they navigate the complex landscape of the region. By recognizing the historical context, the impact of neoliberal policies, and the role of political and social movements, policymakers can develop informed strategies that promote sustainable economic development, social inclusion, and political stability in Latin America.

Import substitution industrialization

Subchapter: Import Substitution Industrialization

Introduction:

In the last half century, Latin America has witnessed significant political, social, and economic changes. One of the notable strategies adopted by several countries in the region during this period was Import Substitution Industrialization (ISI). This subchapter explores the concept of ISI, its objectives, implementation, and its impact on the political, social, and economic landscape of Latin America.

ISI: A Response to Economic Challenges

Facing economic challenges and seeking to reduce dependency on foreign goods, many Latin American countries embraced ISI as a development strategy. The core objective of ISI was to promote domestic industries by substituting imported goods with domestically produced ones. This policy aimed to foster economic self-sufficiency, reduce foreign exchange expenditure, and create employment opportunities within the region.

Implementation of ISI:

To implement ISI, governments adopted a range of measures, including tariffs and trade barriers, subsidies to domestic industries, and restrictions on foreign investment. These policies encouraged the growth of domestic industries, particularly in sectors such as manufacturing, textiles, and automobiles. Governments also provided financial and technical support to local entrepreneurs, fostering innovation and entrepreneurship.

Impact on Political, Social, and Economic Landscape:

ISI had a profound impact on the political, social, and economic aspects of Latin American countries. Economically, ISI led to the growth of domestic industries and diversification of the economy. It provided employment opportunities, reduced dependency on foreign goods, and promoted technological advancements.

However, ISI also faced challenges. The protected domestic industries often lacked international competitiveness, resulting in inefficient production and limited export capabilities. This led to a reliance on state subsidies and protectionist measures, which strained government budgets and hindered long-term economic growth.

Moreover, the social impact of ISI varied across countries. While it contributed to urbanization and the expansion of the middle class, it also exacerbated income inequalities and marginalized rural communities. The political landscape was shaped by the tensions between domestic industries, foreign investors, and social movements advocating for a fair distribution of wealth.

Conclusion:

In conclusion, Import Substitution Industrialization played a significant role in shaping the political, social, and economic changes in Latin America during the last half century. Although it achieved some of its objectives, ISI faced challenges and limitations that prompted a shift towards neoliberal economic policies in later years. Understanding the impact of ISI is crucial for diplomats and politicians working towards sustainable economic development and addressing the social and political challenges faced by Latin American countries.

Debt crisis and structural adjustment programs

Debt crisis and structural adjustment programs have played a significant role in shaping the political, social, and economic changes of Latin America during the last half century. This subchapter aims to provide insights into the complexities of this issue, addressing the audience of diplomats and politicians who are crucial actors in shaping policies in Latin America.

The debt crisis that plagued Latin America in the 1980s had a profound impact on the region's economies. Many countries found themselves unable to service their external debts, leading to a severe economic downturn and social unrest. In response, international financial institutions, such as the International Monetary Fund (IMF) and the World Bank, proposed structural adjustment programs as a condition for financial assistance.

These programs aimed to address the underlying structural issues that contributed to the debt crisis by implementing neoliberal economic policies. The focus was on reducing government intervention in the economy, promoting free trade, and implementing austerity measures. While these policies were intended to stabilize the economies and promote growth, they often came at the expense of social welfare programs and marginalized populations.

Political transitions and democratization processes in Latin America have been closely intertwined with the debt crisis and structural adjustment programs. As countries underwent economic reforms, they also experienced political transitions from authoritarian regimes to democratic systems. These transitions presented both opportunities and challenges for the region, with new governments facing the difficult task of balancing economic stability with social inclusion.

Social movements played a pivotal role in shaping Latin American societies during this period. Movements advocating for indigenous rights, gender equality, and environmental sustainability emerged as powerful forces, challenging the status quo and demanding more inclusive policies. These movements were often met with resistance from governments and powerful elites, leading to social and political tensions.

The rise of populism in Latin America has also been connected to the debt crisis and structural adjustment programs. Populist leaders, capitalizing on popular discontent with the effects of neoliberal policies, gained support by promising to address social inequalities and challenge the influence of international financial institutions. However, the long-term consequences of populism in the region have been mixed, with some countries experiencing economic instability and political polarization.

Foreign intervention has played a significant role in shaping Latin American politics and economies. Historical examples, such as the United States' interventions in Guatemala and Chile, have left lasting scars on the region. The influence of globalization on Latin American economies and cultures cannot be ignored either, as it has brought both opportunities and challenges, including increased trade and investment but also increased inequality and cultural homogenization.

In conclusion, the debt crisis and structural adjustment programs have had a profound impact on Latin America's political, social, and economic landscape. Understanding these complexities is crucial for diplomats and politicians to navigate the challenges and opportunities presented by this transformative period. It is essential to strike a balance between economic stability and social inclusion, recognizing the importance of indigenous rights, gender equality, environmental sustainability, and the role of international organizations in shaping policies.

Neoliberal economic policies and their impact on Latin American economies

Over the past half century, Latin America has witnessed significant political, social, and economic changes. One of the key factors that has shaped the region's economic landscape is the adoption of neoliberal economic policies. This subchapter aims to examine the impact of these policies on Latin American economies, addressing the audience of diplomats and politicians who are invested in understanding the region's economic transformation.

Neoliberalism, characterized by the promotion of free markets, limited government intervention, and privatization, gained popularity in Latin America during the 1980s and 1990s. These policies were implemented as a response to economic crises, high inflation rates, and debt burdens. Advocates argued that neoliberal reforms would attract foreign investment, promote economic growth, and reduce poverty.

However, the impact of neoliberal policies on Latin American economies has been mixed. While some countries experienced economic growth and reduced poverty rates, others faced increased inequality and social unrest. The subchapter will explore these varying outcomes, providing a nuanced analysis of the factors that contributed to success or failure.

Furthermore, it will examine the role of political transitions and democratization processes in shaping the implementation and outcomes of neoliberal policies. The subchapter will highlight the importance of inclusive governance and social dialogue in ensuring that the benefits of economic reforms are widely shared.

Additionally, the subchapter will shed light on the influence of social movements in shaping Latin American societies and their role in challenging the neoliberal agenda. It will discuss the rise of populism in the region and how it has both advanced and hindered progress towards economic development.

Moreover, it will delve into the effects of foreign intervention on Latin American politics and economies, examining the historical context of foreign interference and its impact on economic policies and national sovereignty.

The subchapter will also touch upon the recognition of indigenous rights and the progress made in gender equality and women's empowerment in Latin American countries. It will discuss how these social advancements have intersected with economic policies and contributed to the overall development of the region.

Lastly, the subchapter will highlight the environmental challenges faced by Latin America and the importance of sustainability in economic development. It will explore the role of international organizations in shaping policies that promote sustainable growth and protect the region's natural resources.

In conclusion, this subchapter will provide a comprehensive analysis of the impact of neoliberal economic policies on Latin American economies. By addressing the concerns and interests of diplomats and politicians, it aims to facilitate a deeper understanding of the complex relationship between economic reforms, political transitions, social movements, and the overall development of the region.

Economic diversification and the role of foreign investment

In the last half century, Latin America has witnessed significant political, social, and economic changes. One of the key factors that have driven these changes is the pursuit of economic diversification and the role that foreign investment has played in this process. This subchapter explores the importance of economic diversification and the role that foreign investment has played in shaping Latin America's path to progress.

Economic diversification refers to the process of expanding a country's economy by reducing its dependence on a single sector or industry. In the case of Latin America, this has meant moving away from a heavy reliance on primary commodities, such as oil, minerals, and agriculture, towards a more diversified and robust economy.

Foreign investment has been instrumental in driving this process of economic diversification. It brings in capital, technology, and expertise that are often lacking in domestic industries. Foreign investors are attracted to Latin America's vast market potential, abundant natural resources, and growing consumer base. They have played a crucial role in developing new industries, such as manufacturing, services, and high-tech sectors, which have contributed to job creation, increased productivity, and economic growth.

Furthermore, foreign investment has also facilitated the transfer of knowledge and best practices, helping to improve governance, institutions, and regulatory frameworks. This has resulted in a more favorable business environment, attracting even more foreign investment and fostering a virtuous cycle of economic development.

However, the role of foreign investment in Latin America has not been without challenges. It has been subject to political and economic fluctuations, as well as external shocks. Moreover, concerns have been raised about the potential negative social and environmental impacts of certain foreign investments, such as large-scale infrastructure projects or extractive industries.

Therefore, it is essential for diplomats and politicians to strike a balance between attracting foreign investment and ensuring that it aligns with sustainable development goals. This requires promoting responsible investment practices, protecting the rights of local communities, and safeguarding the environment.

In conclusion, economic diversification and the role of foreign investment have been crucial in shaping Latin America's path to progress in the last half century. While foreign investment has brought numerous benefits, it is essential to address its challenges and ensure that it contributes to sustainable and inclusive development. By doing so, Latin America can continue its journey towards economic prosperity and social well-being.

Chapter 2: The Impact of Neoliberal Economic Policies on Latin American Economies

The Rise of Neoliberalism in Latin America

In the last half century, Latin America has experienced a profound transformation in its political, social, and economic landscape. One of the key driving forces behind these changes has been the rise of neoliberalism. This subchapter will explore the origins, implications, and challenges posed by this ideology in the context of Latin America, addressing a diverse audience of diplomats and politicians.

Neoliberalism, as an economic and political philosophy, gained traction in Latin America during the 1980s and 1990s. Proponents argued that free markets, limited government intervention, and privatization of state-owned enterprises were the keys to economic growth and development. Many Latin American countries, facing economic crises and debt burdens, embraced these policies as a way to attract foreign investment and stimulate their economies.

The impact of neoliberal economic policies on Latin American economies has been a subject of intense debate. While some countries experienced economic growth and stability, others faced rising inequality, social unrest, and even economic collapse. Critics argue that neoliberal reforms have exacerbated poverty, weakened social safety nets, and widened the gap between the rich and the poor. These concerns have fueled social movements and shaped the political landscape of the region.

Political transitions and democratization processes have also played a significant role in shaping Latin America. As countries moved away from authoritarian regimes, neoliberal policies often accompanied the transition to democracy. However, this transition has not been without challenges. The rise of populism, fueled by disenchantment with the outcomes of neoliberalism, has posed both opportunities and threats to democratic governance in the region.

Foreign intervention has also left its mark on Latin American politics and economies. Historically, Latin America has been subject to external influences, ranging from military interventions to economic conditionalities imposed by international financial institutions. These interventions have shaped the region's political and economic trajectory, often with mixed results.

Recognizing the rights of indigenous peoples and promoting gender equality have been important milestones in Latin American societies. Efforts to grant indigenous communities autonomy and recognition of their cultural heritage have gained momentum. Similarly, the region has made significant strides in promoting gender equality and empowering women in various spheres of public and private life.

Latin America also faces environmental challenges and the need for sustainability. The region is home to diverse ecosystems and natural resources, but also faces threats such as deforestation, pollution, and climate change. Balancing economic growth with environmental preservation has become a pressing issue for policymakers.

International organizations have played a critical role in shaping Latin American policies. Organizations such as the United Nations, World Bank, and International Monetary Fund have provided financial assistance, technical expertise, and policy advice to governments in the region. However, the influence of these organizations has also been criticized for their perceived bias towards neoliberal policies and their impact on national sovereignty.

Lastly, globalization has had profound effects on Latin American economies and cultures. The region has become increasingly interconnected with the global economy, leading to both opportunities and challenges. While globalization has opened up new markets and investment opportunities, it has also exposed Latin American countries to economic volatility and cultural homogenization.

In conclusion, the rise of neoliberalism in Latin America has had far-reaching implications for the region's political, social, and economic landscape. Understanding the origins, impacts, and challenges posed by this ideology is crucial for diplomats and politicians involved in shaping Latin American policies. By examining the complex interplay between neoliberalism and other key issues, such as social movements, foreign intervention, indigenous rights, gender equality, environmental sustainability, international organizations, and globalization, policymakers can navigate the complexities of Latin America's path to progress.

Influence of international financial institutions

In the last half century, Latin America has witnessed significant political, social, and economic changes that have shaped the region's trajectory towards progress. One crucial factor that has played a significant role in these transformations is the influence of international financial institutions (IFIs). Addressing diplomats and politicians, this subchapter aims to explore the impact of IFIs and their role in shaping Latin America's path to progress.

International financial institutions, such as the International Monetary Fund (IMF) and the World Bank, have been instrumental in providing financial assistance and guidance to Latin American countries. Through loans, grants, and technical expertise, these institutions have supported governments in implementing economic reforms and development projects. However, the influence of IFIs has not been without controversy and criticism.

One key aspect to consider is the impact of neoliberal economic policies on Latin American economies. IFIs have often advocated for market-oriented policies, privatization, and deregulation, which have had mixed results. While some Latin American countries have experienced economic growth and stability, others have faced increased inequality, poverty, and social unrest. It is essential for diplomats and politicians to critically analyze the consequences of these policies and their implications for social and economic development.

Political transitions and democratization processes in Latin America have also been influenced by international financial institutions. IFIs have provided financial incentives for countries to adopt democratic reforms, improve governance, and strengthen institutions. However, the challenges of consolidating democratic systems in the region have persisted, with issues such as corruption, populism, and social inequality remaining prevalent.

Social movements have played a crucial role in shaping Latin American societies, advocating for indigenous rights, gender equality, and environmental sustainability. IFIs have increasingly recognized the importance of incorporating social and environmental considerations into their policies and projects, aiming to promote social inclusion and sustainable development.

Foreign intervention has had significant effects on Latin American politics and economies. The influence of major global powers, such as the United States, has often shaped the region's political landscape and economic policies. IFIs have been seen by some as a tool for advancing foreign interests, leading to concerns about national sovereignty and economic dependency.

Furthermore, the recognition of indigenous rights and gender equality has been a significant challenge in Latin American countries. IFIs have played a role in promoting these issues, supporting initiatives that aim to empower marginalized groups and promote social justice.

In conclusion, international financial institutions have had a profound influence on Latin America's political, social, and economic changes in the last half century. While they have provided financial assistance and guidance, their impact has been subject to criticism and controversy. Diplomats and politicians must critically evaluate the consequences of IFIs' policies and projects, ensuring that they contribute to sustainable development, social inclusion, and democratic governance in the region.

Privatization of state-owned enterprises

Privatization of State-Owned Enterprises in Latin America

In the last half century, Latin America has witnessed significant changes in its political, social, and economic landscape. One of the key transformations has been the privatization of state-owned enterprises (SOEs). This subchapter explores the impact of privatization on Latin American economies and societies, addressing the concerns and benefits associated with this process.

Privatization refers to the transfer of ownership and control of SOEs from the state to the private sector. It has been touted as a means to improve the efficiency and productivity of these enterprises, stimulate economic growth, attract foreign investment, and reduce the burden on the state budget. However, the privatization process in Latin America has been accompanied by both successes and challenges.

One of the main benefits of privatization has been the increased efficiency and competitiveness of previously state-run enterprises. Privately owned companies tend to be more dynamic and innovative, adopting modern management practices and technologies. This has led to improvements in service quality, cost reduction, and increased consumer choice in sectors such as telecommunications, energy, and transportation.

At the same time, the privatization process has faced criticism for its potential negative social impact. Critics argue that privatization has led to job losses, reduced access to essential services for marginalized populations, and increased inequality. The challenge lies in striking a balance between market efficiency and social equity, ensuring that the benefits of privatization are shared widely.

Diplomats and politicians must consider these concerns when designing and implementing privatization policies. It is crucial to establish regulatory frameworks that protect consumers, promote competition, and safeguard workers' rights. Additionally, governments should invest in social safety nets and retraining programs to mitigate the negative effects of privatization on vulnerable populations.

Furthermore, transparency and accountability are essential in the privatization process to prevent corruption and ensure fair competition. Governments should engage in public consultations and dialogue with civil society organizations to build trust and legitimacy. International organizations can play a crucial role in providing technical assistance and best practices to guide the privatization process.

In conclusion, the privatization of state-owned enterprises has been a significant aspect of Latin America's path to progress in the last half century. The impact of privatization on Latin American economies and societies is complex, with both positive and negative outcomes. Diplomats and politicians must carefully consider the social, economic, and political implications of privatization, striving to strike a balance between market efficiency and social equity. By implementing transparent and accountable privatization policies, Latin American countries can maximize the benefits and mitigate the challenges associated with this process.

Trade liberalization and regional integration

Trade liberalization and regional integration have been key factors in shaping Latin America's path to progress over the last half century. These processes have had profound political, social, and economic implications, often driven by the influence of international organizations and the forces of globalization.

Latin America's journey towards trade liberalization began in the 1980s, as many countries in the region sought to break free from the shackles of protectionism. This shift was driven by the recognition that opening up their economies to international trade would lead to increased competitiveness, economic growth, and job creation. Regional integration initiatives, such as the creation of the Mercosur and the Pacific Alliance, further reinforced this trend, promoting greater economic cooperation and integration among Latin American countries.

The impact of these policies on Latin American economies has been substantial. Trade liberalization has led to increased foreign direct investment, expanded export markets, and the diversification of industries. However, it has also exposed these economies to global economic fluctuations and competition, leading to both gains and challenges.

Political transitions and democratization processes have played a crucial role in facilitating trade liberalization and regional integration. As countries transitioned from authoritarian regimes to democratic systems, they embraced free-market principles and sought to integrate into the global economy. This shift was often accompanied by the adoption of neoliberal economic policies, which emphasized market-oriented reforms, privatization, and deregulation.

Social movements have also played a significant role in shaping Latin American societies during this period. Many of these movements emerged in response to the social and economic inequalities exacerbated by trade liberalization. They have advocated for the rights of marginalized groups, such as indigenous communities and women, and have pushed for greater social justice and inclusion.

The rise of populism in Latin America has challenged the trajectory of trade liberalization and regional integration. Populist leaders have often adopted protectionist measures, prioritizing national interests over regional cooperation. This has led to tensions and setbacks in the integration process, as countries have diverged in their policy approaches.

Foreign intervention has had both positive and negative effects on Latin American politics and economies. While some interventions have supported democratic transitions and economic development, others have fueled instability and inequality. Latin American countries have grappled with finding a balance between sovereignty and international cooperation.

Recognition of indigenous rights and the promotion of gender equality have been important developments in the region. Latin American countries have made significant strides in acknowledging the rights of indigenous communities and empowering women. However, challenges remain in fully implementing these rights and achieving true equality.

Environmental challenges and sustainability have become increasingly important issues in Latin America. The region is home to rich biodiversity and natural resources, but also faces threats such as deforestation, pollution, and climate change. Efforts to promote sustainable development and address these challenges have gained momentum in recent years.

International organizations have played a crucial role in shaping Latin American policies. Organizations such as the World Bank, the International Monetary Fund, and the United Nations have provided financial assistance, technical expertise, and policy advice. Their influence has been both welcomed and criticized, as Latin American countries navigate the complexities of global governance and sovereignty.

In conclusion, trade liberalization and regional integration have been central to Latin America's path to progress over the last half century. These processes have had wide-ranging effects on politics, society, and the economy. As Latin America continues to evolve, it will grapple with the opportunities and challenges presented by globalization, while striving for sustainable and inclusive development. Diplomats and politicians must navigate these complex dynamics to ensure the region's continued progress.

Economic Consequences of Neoliberalism

Title: Economic Consequences of Neoliberalism: An In-depth Analysis of Latin America's Path to Progress

Introduction:

In this subchapter, we delve into the economic consequences of neoliberalism in Latin America, exploring its impact on the region's development over the last half century. This analysis is crucial for diplomats and politicians seeking a comprehensive understanding of the challenges and opportunities Latin America faces today. By examining the socio-economic changes, political transitions, and the influence of international organizations and globalization, we can gain valuable insights to shape policies that promote sustainable progress.

Neoliberalism and Latin America:

Neoliberal economic policies, largely embraced in Latin America during the 1980s and 1990s, had profound consequences on the region's economies. The implementation of austerity measures, privatization, and deregulation aimed to promote economic growth and attract foreign investment. However, the outcomes were mixed, with some countries experiencing rapid development, while others faced increased inequality, poverty, and social unrest.

Impact on Latin American Economies:

Neoliberal policies resulted in significant shifts in Latin American economies. The opening of markets and trade liberalization led to increased integration with the global economy, creating both opportunities and challenges. While some countries became more competitive, others struggled to adapt, leading to uneven development and vulnerability to external shocks. Income disparities widened, exacerbating social inequality and hindering sustainable development.

Political Transitions and Democratization Processes:

Neoliberalism coincided with political transitions and democratization processes in Latin America. The adoption of market-oriented reforms often occurred alongside political changes, as countries sought to consolidate democratic governance. However, the implementation of neoliberal policies sometimes strained social cohesion, leading to political polarization and the rise of populism.

Social Movements and Their Role:

Amidst the economic changes, social movements played a crucial role in shaping Latin American societies. Grassroots organizations advocating for indigenous rights, gender equality, and environmental sustainability emerged. These movements challenged the neoliberal model, demanding greater social inclusion, participatory democracy, and sustainable development.

Foreign Intervention and Indigenous Rights:

The effects of foreign intervention on Latin American politics and economies cannot be overlooked. Historical patterns of intervention often undermined local economies and political stability. Furthermore, the recognition of indigenous rights became a key issue, as marginalized communities sought to protect their lands, cultures, and livelihoods from external forces.

Conclusion:

The economic consequences of neoliberalism in Latin America have been wide-ranging. While some countries have reaped the benefits of market-oriented reforms, others continue to grapple with persistent challenges such as inequality, poverty, and environmental degradation. Diplomats and politicians must consider this complex landscape when formulating policies that address the region's pressing issues, including social inclusion, sustainable development, and democratic governance. By understanding the historical context and current dynamics, we can collectively shape Latin America's path to progress.

Income inequality and wealth concentration

Income inequality and wealth concentration have been longstanding challenges in Latin America, shaping the political, social, and economic landscape of the region over the last half century. As diplomats and politicians, it is crucial to understand the complexities and consequences of these issues in order to effectively address them and promote inclusive and sustainable development.

Latin America has historically been one of the most unequal regions in the world, with a small elite controlling a disproportionate share of wealth and power. The concentration of wealth not only perpetuates social divisions but also hampers economic growth and undermines democratic institutions. High levels of income inequality have led to social unrest, political instability, and a lack of social cohesion, hindering progress in other areas such as education, healthcare, and infrastructure.

The impact of neoliberal economic policies on Latin American economies has been a key factor contributing to income inequality. The implementation of market-oriented reforms, often under the influence of international financial institutions, has led to the dismantling of welfare systems, privatization of public services, and deregulation of labor markets. While these policies have aimed to promote economic growth, they have often exacerbated inequalities by favoring the wealthy elite and neglecting the needs of the most vulnerable populations.

Political transitions and democratization processes in Latin America have played a crucial role in addressing income inequality and wealth concentration. The region has witnessed a shift towards more inclusive and participatory democracies, with increased recognition of human rights and social justice. Governments have implemented redistributive policies, such as cash transfer programs and progressive taxation, to reduce inequality and improve social outcomes. However, progress has been uneven, and challenges remain in ensuring that these policies are sustainable and reach the most marginalized communities.

Social movements have played a pivotal role in shaping Latin American societies and advocating for greater equality. Movements such as indigenous rights, women's empowerment, and environmental sustainability have gained traction and influenced policy agendas. These movements have challenged traditional power structures and pushed for more inclusive and equitable societies. Diverse voices and perspectives must be included in decision-making processes to ensure that policies effectively address the root causes of income inequality and wealth concentration.

Foreign intervention and globalization have also had profound effects on Latin American politics and economies. Historical patterns of colonialism, imperialism, and economic exploitation have perpetuated inequalities and hindered sustainable development. Addressing income inequality and wealth concentration requires not only domestic reforms but also a global commitment to fair trade, debt relief, and the promotion of equitable international relations.

In conclusion, income inequality and wealth concentration are critical issues that have shaped Latin America's path to progress over the last half century. By understanding the root causes of these challenges and considering their social, political, and economic implications, diplomats and politicians can work towards promoting inclusive and sustainable development in the region. This requires implementing redistributive policies, empowering marginalized groups, and fostering international cooperation to address the systemic inequalities that continue to persist in Latin America.

Economic instability and financial crises

Economic instability and financial crises have been recurring challenges that Latin America has faced throughout the last half century. These crises have had profound consequences on the political, social, and economic landscape of the region. In this subchapter, we will explore the causes and impacts of economic instability and financial crises in

Latin America, and the efforts made to address and mitigate these challenges.

Latin America has experienced several economic crises over the past decades, often characterized by high inflation rates, currency devaluations, and unsustainable levels of public debt. These crises have been influenced by a variety of factors, including external shocks, such as fluctuations in commodity prices, and internal structural issues, such as inadequate fiscal policies and weak financial systems.

The impact of neoliberal economic policies, which gained prominence in the 1980s, on Latin American economies cannot be overlooked in the context of economic instability. While these policies aimed to promote market-oriented reforms and attract foreign investment, they also led to the dismantling of social safety nets and the exacerbation of income inequality. As a result, social discontent grew, leading to widespread social movements and protests against these policies.

Political transitions and democratization processes have also played a significant role in shaping the economic stability of Latin American countries. The region has witnessed a wave of transitions from military dictatorships to democratic governments. However, the consolidation of democracy has not always translated into economic stability, as many countries have struggled to tackle corruption, strengthen institutions, and implement effective governance mechanisms.

The rise of populism in Latin America has further complicated the economic stability of the region. Populist leaders, often with charismatic personalities, have promised rapid economic growth and social inclusion but have often pursued unsustainable economic policies, leading to further instability and crises.

Foreign intervention has had a profound impact on Latin American politics and economies. Historical examples, such as the United States' involvement in the region during the Cold War, have shaped the trajectory of political and economic development. These interventions have often prioritized geopolitical interests over the well-being of local populations, exacerbating economic instability.

Recognizing and addressing the rights of indigenous communities and promoting gender equality have also been critical for achieving economic stability in Latin America. These issues have historically been overlooked, leading to social exclusion and economic inequality. Efforts to promote indigenous rights and gender equality have been essential in creating more inclusive and sustainable economies.

Furthermore, Latin America faces significant environmental challenges, including deforestation, pollution, and climate change. These challenges have economic implications, affecting industries such as agriculture and tourism. Sustainable development strategies and policies are crucial for ensuring the long-term economic stability of the region.

International organizations have played a crucial role in shaping Latin American policies. Institutions such as the International Monetary Fund (IMF) and the World Bank have provided financial assistance and policy advice during times of crises. However, these organizations have also faced criticism for imposing stringent conditions that exacerbate social inequalities.

Lastly, the influence of globalization on Latin American economies and cultures cannot be ignored. Globalization has brought both opportunities and challenges. While it has facilitated trade and investment, it has also exposed the region to economic volatility and cultural homogenization.

In conclusion, economic instability and financial crises have been persistent challenges for Latin America over the last half century. These crises have been influenced by a multitude of factors, including neoliberal economic policies, political transitions, social movements, foreign intervention, and environmental challenges. Addressing these issues and promoting inclusive and sustainable economic growth are essential for the region's progress and stability.

Dependency on foreign capital and resources

Latin America has long been characterized by its dependence on foreign capital and resources. This subchapter aims to explore the various aspects of this dependency and its implications for the political, social, and economic changes that have taken place in the region over the last half century.

One of the key factors contributing to Latin America's dependency on foreign capital is the region's historical reliance on exports of primary commodities, such as oil, minerals, and agricultural products. This reliance has made Latin American economies vulnerable to fluctuations in global commodity prices and has hindered their ability to diversify and develop more sustainable industries.

Furthermore, Latin America has often turned to foreign capital to finance its development projects and address fiscal deficits. However, this has come at a cost. Foreign investment often comes with conditions, such as privatization of state-owned enterprises and deregulation of markets, which have had significant social and economic consequences for the region.

The impact of neoliberal economic policies on Latin American economies cannot be understated. In the pursuit of attracting foreign investment, many Latin American countries implemented market-oriented reforms that prioritized free trade, deregulation, and privatization. While these policies were intended to promote economic growth and development, they often exacerbated inequality, increased poverty rates, and weakened the social safety nets in the region.

Political transitions and democratization processes in Latin America have also been influenced by foreign intervention. During the Cold War, Latin America became a battleground for competing ideologies, with the United States supporting authoritarian regimes to counter the spread of communism. This intervention had long-lasting effects on the region's political landscape, with many countries experiencing prolonged periods of authoritarian rule and political instability.

Social movements have played a crucial role in shaping Latin American societies and challenging foreign intervention. From indigenous rights movements to feminist movements, these grassroots organizations have advocated for social justice, equality, and the recognition of marginalized groups. Their efforts have not only influenced policy changes but have also contributed to the democratization processes in the region.

The rise of populism in Latin America can also be seen as a response to the region's dependency on foreign capital and resources. Populist leaders have often used nationalist rhetoric to challenge the influence of foreign powers and prioritize the interests of the domestic population. While populism has had mixed results in Latin America, it highlights the deep-rooted issues of inequality, corruption, and social exclusion that persist in the region.

In conclusion, Latin America's dependency on foreign capital and resources has shaped the political, social, and economic changes that have taken place in the region over the last half century. From the impact of neoliberal economic policies to the influence of foreign intervention, these dynamics have had profound implications for the development and sustainability of Latin American countries. Understanding and addressing this dependency is crucial for diplomats and politicians seeking to promote progress and prosperity in the region.

Chapter 3: Political Transitions and Democratization Processes in Latin America

Transition from Authoritarian Rule to Democracy

In the last half century, Latin America has witnessed significant political, social, and economic changes, including the transition from authoritarian rule to democracy. This subchapter explores the dynamics and challenges faced during this crucial period of transition, highlighting the impact on the region's political, social, and economic landscapes.

The transition from authoritarian rule to democracy in Latin America has been a complex and multifaceted process. It has involved the dismantling of repressive regimes, the establishment of democratic institutions, and the promotion of human rights and civil liberties. Diplomats and politicians must understand the intricacies of this transition to effectively engage with Latin American countries and support their democratic development.

Political transitions and democratization processes in Latin America have been marked by both successes and challenges. While many countries have successfully transitioned to democratic systems, others have faced setbacks and struggled with issues such as corruption, weak institutions, and political instability. Diplomats and politicians need to be aware of these challenges and work towards promoting democratic values and institutions in the region.

Social movements have played a crucial role in shaping Latin American societies during the transition to democracy. From labor movements to indigenous rights activists, these social movements have advocated for social justice, equality, and inclusion. Their voices and demands have contributed to the strengthening of democracy and the recognition of marginalized groups in Latin American countries.

The rise of populism in Latin America has also been a significant factor in the transition to democracy. Populist leaders have capitalized on popular discontent with established political parties and institutions, promising radical change and challenging the traditional political elites. Diplomats and politicians must understand the implications of populism for democratic governance and work towards fostering inclusive and accountable political systems.

Foreign intervention has had a profound impact on Latin American politics and economies throughout the transition to democracy. From military interventions to economic policies imposed by international financial institutions, external actors have shaped the region's development trajectory. Diplomats and politicians must navigate the complexities of foreign intervention, ensuring that it promotes democratic values and sustainable economic growth.

Recognition of indigenous rights and gender equality has been a crucial aspect of the transition to democracy in Latin America. Diplomats and politicians must advocate for the inclusion and empowerment of these marginalized groups, promoting policies that address their specific needs and challenges.

As Latin America faces environmental challenges and strives for sustainability, diplomats and politicians must engage with the region on issues such as deforestation, climate change, and natural resource management. They must work towards promoting sustainable development practices that balance economic growth with environmental conservation.

International organizations play a pivotal role in shaping Latin American policies and supporting democratic transitions. From the

Organization of American States to the United Nations, these organizations provide a platform for dialogue, cooperation, and assistance. Diplomats and politicians must leverage these institutions to promote democratic values, social progress, and economic development in the region.

Finally, the influence of globalization on Latin American economies and cultures has been profound. Diplomats and politicians must navigate the challenges and opportunities presented by globalization, ensuring that it benefits all segments of society and promotes inclusive and sustainable development.

In conclusion, the transition from authoritarian rule to democracy in Latin America has been a complex and multifaceted process. Diplomats and politicians must understand the dynamics and challenges of this transition to effectively engage with the region and support its democratic development. By promoting democratic values, inclusive policies, and sustainable development, they can contribute to Latin America's path to progress.

The role of civil society and human rights movements

The role of civil society and human rights movements in Latin America's Path to Progress

Introduction:

Throughout the last half century, Latin America has undergone significant political, social, and economic changes. These changes have been shaped, to a great extent, by the active participation of civil society and human rights movements. This subchapter will explore the crucial role that these movements have played in driving progress in the region. It will discuss their impact on political transitions, social changes, and economic development, shedding light on their influence on Latin American societies.

Political Transitions and Democratization:

Civil society and human rights movements have been instrumental in driving political transitions and democratization processes in Latin America. These movements have fought against authoritarian regimes, demanding democratic reforms and an end to political repression. Their persistent activism has led to the establishment of democratic governments and the protection of human rights across the region. This subchapter will analyze specific examples of successful transitions and highlight the challenges faced by these movements in confronting entrenched power structures.

Social Movements and Shaping Latin American Societies:

Social movements, such as labor unions, indigenous rights movements, and feminist organizations, have played a vital role in shaping Latin American societies. They have championed the rights of marginalized groups and fought for social justice. This subchapter will delve into the impact of these movements on issues such as indigenous rights, gender equality, and environmental sustainability. It will also explore the challenges faced by these movements in maintaining their progress and the strategies they have employed to overcome obstacles.

Economic Changes and Neoliberal Policies:

The impact of neoliberal economic policies on Latin American economies has been a subject of great debate. Civil society and human rights movements have played a significant role in this discussion, advocating for more inclusive and sustainable economic models. This subchapter will analyze the influence of these movements on economic policies, exploring alternative approaches to development and their potential for long-term prosperity.

Conclusion:

The role of civil society and human rights movements in Latin America's path to progress cannot be overstated. Their activism has shaped political transitions, driven social changes, and influenced economic policies. This subchapter has provided a comprehensive overview of their impact on various aspects of Latin American societies. It has highlighted the challenges they face and the strategies they employ to overcome them. By understanding the pivotal role of civil society and human rights movements, diplomats and politicians can work towards creating more inclusive and sustainable policies that benefit all segments of society.

Truth and reconciliation commissions

Truth and Reconciliation Commissions in Latin America: Towards Healing and Justice

In the wake of political turmoil, human rights abuses, and social conflict, Latin American countries have turned to Truth and Reconciliation Commissions (TRCs) as a means to address the dark chapters of their past. These commissions are an essential component of the region's path to progress, fostering political, social, and economic changes over the last half-century.

TRCs emerged in Latin America as a response to decades of authoritarian rule, civil wars, and systemic human rights violations. Their purpose is to uncover the truth, promote reconciliation, and ensure justice for victims and their families. By investigating and documenting past atrocities, TRCs play a vital role in acknowledging the suffering of individuals and communities, fostering healing, and preventing the recurrence of violence.

The impact of neoliberal economic policies on Latin American economies cannot be discussed without recognizing the role TRCs have played. By addressing historical injustices, these commissions have contributed to the rebuilding of trust and social cohesion, creating a more stable environment for economic growth and development. The truth-seeking process has shed light on the economic inequalities and systemic injustices that hindered progress, prompting policymakers to implement more inclusive and equitable economic policies.

Political transitions and democratization processes in Latin America have been significantly influenced by TRCs. These commissions have helped dismantle the structures of power that perpetuated authoritarianism and paved the way for democratic reforms. By exposing the truth and holding perpetrators accountable, TRCs have empowered civil society and strengthened democratic institutions, ensuring that citizens have a voice in shaping their country's future.

Social movements have played a crucial role in shaping Latin American societies, and TRCs have provided a platform for marginalized groups to have their voices heard. These commissions have given indigenous communities, women, and other vulnerable populations an opportunity to share their experiences and demand justice. By recognizing indigenous rights and promoting gender equality, TRCs have contributed to a more inclusive and diverse society.

The rise of populism in Latin America has posed challenges to truth and reconciliation efforts. Some populist leaders have sought to undermine the work of TRCs, denying the existence of past human rights violations or using them for political gain. However, the resilience of civil society and the commitment of diplomats and politicians to the truth-seeking process have continued to drive progress.

Foreign intervention has long influenced Latin American politics and economies, often exacerbating existing tensions. TRCs provide a framework for addressing the consequences of foreign intervention, acknowledging the role played by external actors in perpetuating conflicts and human rights abuses. By doing so, these commissions contribute to a more balanced and informed understanding of the region's history.

In conclusion, Truth and Reconciliation Commissions have played a pivotal role in Latin America's path to progress over the last half-century. By uncovering the truth, promoting justice, and fostering reconciliation, these commissions have contributed to political, social, and economic changes in the region. As diplomats and politicians, it is crucial to support and strengthen the work of TRCs, recognizing their significance in shaping Latin American policies and ensuring a more just and inclusive future.

Challenges in consolidating democratic institutions

Introduction:

The consolidation of democratic institutions in Latin America has been a complex and multifaceted process. While the region has made significant progress in the last half century, there are still numerous challenges that diplomats and politicians need to address in order to ensure the stability and longevity of these institutions. This subchapter will explore the various challenges faced in consolidating democratic institutions in Latin America.

1. Weak Institutions and Corruption:

One of the key challenges in consolidating democratic institutions in Latin America is the presence of weak institutions and widespread corruption. Many countries in the region struggle with weak rule of law, lack of transparency, and pervasive corruption, which undermine the functioning of democratic institutions. Diplomats and politicians need to work towards strengthening institutions, promoting accountability, and implementing anti-corruption measures to ensure the legitimacy and effectiveness of democratic governance.

2. Political Fragmentation and Polarization:

Latin America has witnessed political fragmentation and polarization, which pose significant challenges to democratic consolidation. Divisive ideologies, party fragmentation, and social polarization hinder effective governance and compromise the ability of democratic institutions to address the needs and aspirations of the population. Diplomats and politicians must foster dialogue, promote consensus-building, and work towards bridging political divides to strengthen democratic institutions.

3. Social Inequality and Exclusion:

Persistent social inequality and exclusion remain major challenges in consolidating democratic institutions in Latin America. The region continues to face high levels of poverty, income inequality, and marginalization of certain social groups. Diplomats and politicians need to prioritize inclusive policies, social welfare programs, and equitable distribution of resources to address these challenges and ensure that democratic institutions serve the interests of all citizens.

4. Populist Threats:

The rise of populism in Latin America presents a significant challenge to democratic consolidation. Populist leaders often undermine democratic institutions, erode the separation of powers, and limit political freedoms. Diplomats and politicians must promote democratic values, defend the rule of law, and combat populist rhetoric to safeguard democratic institutions.

Conclusion:

Consolidating democratic institutions in Latin America requires addressing various challenges such as weak institutions, corruption, political fragmentation, social inequality, and the rise of populism.

Diplomats and politicians play a crucial role in overcoming these challenges by promoting accountability, fostering dialogue, implementing inclusive policies, and defending democratic values. Only through concerted efforts can Latin America continue its path to progress and ensure the stability and longevity of its democratic institutions.

Chapter 4: Social Movements and Their Role in Shaping Latin American Societies

Indigenous Movements and Indigenous Rights

In the last half century, Latin America has witnessed a significant rise in indigenous movements advocating for the recognition and protection of their rights. These movements have played a crucial role in shaping Latin American societies and challenging the historical marginalization and discrimination faced by indigenous communities.

The struggle for indigenous rights in Latin America can be traced back to the colonial era, when the native populations were subjected to forced labor, cultural assimilation, and land dispossession. However, it was only in the latter half of the 20th century that indigenous movements gained momentum and started to make significant strides towards achieving their rights.

One of the key demands of indigenous movements has been the recognition of their ancestral lands and territories. Many indigenous communities have been displaced from their traditional lands due to large-scale development projects, extractive industries, and agricultural expansion. These movements have fought for land rights and the demarcation of indigenous territories, aiming to preserve their cultural heritage and maintain sustainable livelihoods.

Additionally, indigenous movements have been at the forefront of advocating for cultural rights and the recognition of indigenous languages, customs, and traditions. They have pushed for greater inclusion and participation in decision-making processes, both at the national and international levels. This has led to the adoption of important legal frameworks, such as the United Nations Declaration on the Rights of Indigenous Peoples, which has provided a solid foundation for the protection and promotion of indigenous rights in Latin America.

The recognition of indigenous rights has not only been a moral imperative but also crucial for sustainable development and social cohesion in Latin America. Indigenous communities possess valuable knowledge and practices that can contribute to environmental conservation, sustainable resource management, and the preservation of biodiversity. Their inclusion in policy-making processes is therefore essential for achieving long-term social, economic, and environmental progress in the region.

Despite the progress made, challenges remain in fully implementing indigenous rights in Latin America. Indigenous communities continue to face discrimination, violence, and unequal access to basic services such as education and healthcare. Furthermore, the extractive industries and large-scale infrastructure projects that often threaten indigenous territories persist, highlighting the ongoing struggle for the protection of indigenous rights.

As diplomats and politicians, it is crucial to recognize and support the indigenous movements in Latin America. By promoting inclusive policies and working towards the full recognition of indigenous rights, we can contribute to a more just and equitable society, where all individuals, regardless of their cultural background, can fully participate and benefit from the region's political, social, and economic progress.

Recognition of indigenous cultures and languages

In the last half century, Latin America has experienced significant political, social, and economic changes. One important aspect of these changes is the recognition of indigenous cultures and languages. This subchapter will explore the progress made in acknowledging and valuing the rich diversity of indigenous communities in Latin America.

Indigenous cultures and languages have long been marginalized and overlooked in Latin American societies. However, in recent years, there has been a growing awareness and appreciation for the unique contributions and perspectives that indigenous communities bring to the region. Diplomats and politicians have played a crucial role in advocating for the recognition of indigenous rights and promoting policies that support their cultural preservation.

One key development in this area has been the establishment of legal protections for indigenous peoples. Many Latin American countries have enacted legislation that guarantees the rights of indigenous communities, including the right to maintain and develop their own cultures, languages, and traditional knowledge. These laws also promote political representation and participation for indigenous peoples, ensuring their voices are heard in decision-making processes.

Furthermore, there has been a greater emphasis on bilingual education programs that aim to preserve indigenous languages while providing access to mainstream education. This recognition of indigenous languages as valuable cultural assets helps to combat the historical marginalization and discrimination faced by indigenous communities.

The recognition of indigenous cultures and languages has also had a profound impact on shaping Latin American societies. It has fostered a sense of pride and identity among indigenous communities, leading to increased political mobilization and social activism. Indigenous movements have played a pivotal role in advocating for their rights, challenging discriminatory practices, and demanding greater inclusion in political and economic processes.

The recognition of indigenous cultures and languages also intersects with other important issues in Latin America, such as gender equality, environmental challenges, and the influence of globalization. Indigenous women have been at the forefront of advocating for both indigenous and women's rights, highlighting the intersectionality of these struggles. Additionally, indigenous communities have been key actors in the fight against climate change and the preservation of natural resources, as their territories often contain vital ecosystems.

In conclusion, the recognition of indigenous cultures and languages in Latin America is a vital component of the region's path to progress. Diplomats and politicians have a crucial role to play in supporting policies that value and protect the rights of indigenous communities. By acknowledging and embracing the rich diversity of indigenous cultures and languages, Latin America can build a more inclusive and equitable society that truly reflects the region's vibrant heritage.

Land rights and territorial autonomy

Land rights and territorial autonomy have been crucial issues in Latin America's path to progress over the last half century. These topics are of great relevance to diplomats and politicians, as they directly impact the political, social, and economic changes in the region.

Throughout history, Latin America has faced numerous challenges in terms of land ownership and control. The legacy of colonialism and the concentration of land in the hands of a few elites have created deep inequalities and social unrest. Recognizing the importance of land rights, many Latin American countries have undertaken significant efforts to address this issue and promote territorial autonomy.

One key aspect of this process has been the recognition of indigenous rights. Indigenous communities have historically been marginalized and excluded from decision-making processes regarding their lands. However, in recent years, there has been a growing recognition of their rights and the importance of their traditional territories. This has led to the implementation of policies that aim to protect their land rights and promote their territorial autonomy.

Furthermore, gender equality and women's empowerment have also played a crucial role in the fight for land rights and territorial autonomy. Women, particularly indigenous women, have been at the forefront of social movements advocating for land rights and have played a crucial role in shaping Latin American societies. Their participation in decision-making processes has been key to achieving meaningful progress in this area.

The recognition of land rights and territorial autonomy is not only a matter of social justice but also has important economic implications. Sustainable land management and the protection of natural resources are vital for the region's development. By recognizing the rights of communities to their lands, Latin American countries can promote sustainable practices and enhance environmental protection.

International organizations have also played a significant role in shaping policies related to land rights and territorial autonomy in Latin America. These organizations have provided support, technical assistance, and funding to promote sustainable land management, indigenous rights, and gender equality.

In conclusion, land rights and territorial autonomy are crucial issues that have shaped the political, social, and economic changes in Latin America over the last half century. Recognizing the rights of indigenous communities, promoting gender equality, and implementing sustainable land management practices are key steps towards achieving progress in this area. The involvement of international organizations and the collaboration between diplomats and politicians are essential for addressing these challenges and promoting a more inclusive and sustainable future for Latin America.

Representation in politics and decision-making processes

In the past half century, Latin America has witnessed significant political, social, and economic changes that have reshaped the region's trajectory. One crucial aspect of this transformation is the issue of representation in politics and decision-making processes. This subchapter explores the progress made in this area and the challenges that remain, addressing the diplomats and politicians who have the power to drive further change.

Democratization processes have been at the forefront of Latin America's political landscape, with many countries transitioning from authoritarian regimes to democratic systems. However, true representation of all segments of society is still a work in progress. While the region has made significant strides in increasing political participation and representation, there is still a need to ensure that marginalized groups, such as indigenous communities and women, have an equal voice in decision-making processes.

Social movements have played a crucial role in shaping Latin American societies and pushing for greater representation. These movements have advocated for the recognition of indigenous rights, gender equality, and environmental sustainability. Their demands have forced politicians to address the needs and aspirations of these marginalized groups, leading to policy changes and constitutional reforms.

The rise of populism in Latin America has also had an impact on representation in politics. Populist leaders have often presented themselves as champions of the people, appealing to the frustrations of those who feel excluded from the political process. However, the challenge lies in ensuring that populist movements do not undermine democratic institutions and that representation remains inclusive and accountable.

Foreign intervention has also shaped Latin American politics and economies, often influencing decision-making processes. While some interventions have had positive effects, such as promoting human rights and democracy, others have been detrimental, leading to political instability and economic dependency. Latin American diplomats and politicians must navigate the complex dynamics of foreign intervention to protect their countries' interests and ensure the representation of their citizens.

In conclusion, representation in politics and decision-making processes is a crucial aspect of Latin America's path to progress. While significant strides have been made, there is still much work to be done to ensure the inclusion and empowerment of all segments of society. Diplomats and politicians must continue to advocate for the rights of marginalized groups, address the challenges posed by populism and foreign intervention, and work towards a more inclusive and representative political system. Only through these efforts can Latin America achieve sustainable political, social, and economic development in the coming decades.

Women's Movements and Gender Equality

In the last half century, Latin America has witnessed significant advancements in women's movements and gender equality. This subchapter explores the progress made, challenges faced, and the importance of continuing efforts in achieving gender equality in the region.

Latin America's women's movements have played a crucial role in challenging traditional gender norms and advocating for women's rights. These movements have pushed for legal reforms and policies to address gender-based violence, discrimination, and unequal access to education, healthcare, and economic opportunities.

The impact of women's movements and gender equality initiatives has been far-reaching. Increased participation of women in politics and decision-making positions has led to more inclusive policies and legislation that address women's needs and concerns. For example, countries like Argentina, Chile, and Bolivia have implemented gender quotas, ensuring greater representation of women in political and public spheres.

However, challenges persist. Gender-based violence remains prevalent, with femicide rates alarmingly high in some countries. Additionally, women continue to face barriers in accessing education, healthcare, and economic opportunities, perpetuating gender inequality. Addressing these challenges requires comprehensive strategies that involve legal reforms, awareness campaigns, and targeted policies to promote women's empowerment.

Diplomats and politicians must recognize the importance of promoting gender equality as a fundamental aspect of sustainable development. By prioritizing women's rights, policymakers can foster inclusive societies, strengthen democracy, and promote economic growth. Moreover, promoting gender equality is not only a matter of social justice but also a smart economic choice, as studies have shown that gender equality correlates with increased productivity and economic prosperity.

International organizations have a crucial role to play in shaping policies and supporting initiatives that advance gender equality. They can provide technical assistance, funding, and expertise to governments and civil society organizations working towards women's empowerment. Moreover, international cooperation and dialogue can facilitate the exchange of best practices and lessons learned from different countries.

In conclusion, women's movements and gender equality have made significant strides in Latin America in the last half century. However, challenges remain, and continuous efforts are necessary to achieve full gender equality. Diplomats and politicians must prioritize women's rights and empowerment as an integral part of political, social, and economic progress in the region. Through collaboration, policy reforms, and international cooperation, Latin America can continue its path towards a more inclusive and equal society for all.

Legal reforms and gender quotas

Legal reforms and gender quotas have played a crucial role in shaping Latin America's path to progress in the last half century. These reforms have been instrumental in addressing gender inequality and promoting women's empowerment in the region. This subchapter explores the significant changes that legal reforms and gender quotas have brought about in Latin America, focusing on their impact on politics, society, and the economy.

In recent decades, Latin America has witnessed a growing recognition of the need for gender equality and women's empowerment. This has led to the implementation of legal reforms aimed at ensuring equal rights and opportunities for women in various spheres of life. One of the most significant reforms has been the introduction of gender quotas in political representation. Many countries in the region have adopted laws that mandate a certain percentage of women in legislative bodies, political parties, and other decision-making positions. These quotas have proven effective in increasing women's political participation and representation, challenging traditional gender roles, and fostering a more inclusive and democratic political landscape.

The impact of gender quotas extends beyond politics. It has also contributed to significant social changes in Latin American societies. By challenging traditional gender norms and empowering women, these reforms have paved the way for greater gender equality in education, employment, and access to healthcare. They have also played a crucial role in combating violence against women and promoting women's rights.

Moreover, legal reforms and gender quotas have had economic implications. Studies have shown that gender equality can boost economic growth and reduce poverty. By increasing women's participation in the labor force and promoting their entrepreneurship, these reforms have contributed to the region's economic development. They have also helped address income inequality and promote social cohesion.

However, challenges remain in fully implementing and enforcing these legal reforms. Deep-rooted cultural norms, gender stereotypes, and resistance from conservative groups have hindered progress in some countries. Additionally, there is a need for comprehensive policies that address the intersecting inequalities faced by women, such as race, class, and indigenous heritage.

In conclusion, legal reforms and gender quotas have been crucial in promoting gender equality and women's empowerment in Latin America. These reforms have brought about significant changes in politics, society, and the economy. However, further efforts are needed to overcome the remaining challenges and ensure the full realization of gender equality in the region. Diplomats and politicians play a crucial role in advocating for and supporting these reforms, as they have the power to influence policy-making and shape the future of Latin America.

Violence against women and femicide

Violence against women and femicide have been longstanding issues in Latin America, posing considerable challenges to the region's progress in political, social, and economic spheres. This subchapter aims to shed light on the extent of these problems, their underlying causes, and potential solutions that diplomats and politicians can consider in their pursuit of a more equitable and just Latin America.

Latin America has long grappled with high rates of violence against women and femicide, which refers to the intentional killing of women due to their gender. This pervasive issue is deeply rooted in patriarchal norms, gender inequality, and a culture of machismo that perpetuate the subordination and objectification of women. Such violence not only violates women's fundamental rights but also hampers their ability to participate fully in political, social, and economic life.

The consequences of violence against women and femicide are far-reaching. They include not only physical and psychological harm to individuals but also broader impacts on families, communities, and societies as a whole. These issues hinder the progress of Latin America by impeding gender equality, undermining social cohesion, and limiting women's contributions to economic development.

Addressing violence against women and femicide requires a comprehensive approach that tackles both the symptoms and the underlying causes. This includes implementing legal frameworks that protect women's rights, ensuring effective law enforcement and judicial systems, and promoting gender-sensitive education that challenges harmful gender norms. Additionally, promoting women's empowerment and facilitating their economic inclusion are crucial in breaking the cycle of violence and fostering long-term change.

International cooperation and collaboration are essential in combating violence against women and femicide in Latin America. Diplomats and politicians can play a crucial role in advocating for gender equality, supporting local initiatives, and fostering regional dialogue on these issues. By prioritizing this subchapter's recommendations, policymakers can contribute to creating a safer and more inclusive Latin America, where women can exercise their rights freely and participate fully in all aspects of society.

In conclusion, violence against women and femicide remain significant challenges in Latin America. Tackling these issues requires a multi-faceted approach that addresses the root causes, promotes gender equality, and empowers women. By prioritizing this subchapter's recommendations, diplomats and politicians can contribute to a more progressive and equitable Latin America.

Economic empowerment and access to education

Economic Empowerment and Access to Education in Latin America

In the last half-century, Latin America has witnessed significant political, social, and economic changes. One of the key areas that has seen tremendous progress is the issue of economic empowerment and access to education. This subchapter explores the strides that have been made in these areas and the challenges that still remain.

Access to education is a fundamental right that is crucial for the development of individuals and societies. In Latin America, efforts have been made to ensure that education is accessible to all, regardless of socio-economic background. Governments have implemented policies to increase enrollment rates and reduce dropout rates, with a focus on marginalized communities.

However, despite these efforts, challenges persist. Quality education remains elusive for many, particularly in rural and remote areas. Inequities in educational opportunities still exist, perpetuating social and economic disparities. To address these challenges, policymakers need to prioritize investment in education, ensure teacher training and support, and promote innovative approaches to learning.

Economic empowerment is another crucial aspect that has seen progress in Latin America. The region has experienced significant economic growth and poverty reduction in recent years. This has been achieved through the implementation of neoliberal economic policies that promote free markets, foreign investment, and trade liberalization.

However, the impact of these policies has been mixed. While they have contributed to economic growth, they have also resulted in income inequality and the concentration of wealth in the hands of a few. It is essential for governments to strike a balance between economic growth and social inclusion, ensuring that the benefits of development are shared equitably.

Furthermore, economic empowerment cannot be achieved without addressing gender inequality. Women's empowerment has gained traction in Latin America, with increased recognition of their rights and participation in decision-making processes. However, significant challenges persist, including gender-based violence and discrimination. Policymakers need to prioritize gender equality and create an enabling environment for women's economic participation.

In conclusion, Latin America has made significant strides in economic empowerment and access to education in the last half-century. However, challenges remain, and policymakers need to continue their efforts to ensure that education is accessible to all and economic empowerment is inclusive. By addressing these issues, Latin America can pave the path to progress and create a more equitable and prosperous future for its citizens. Diplomats and politicians play a crucial role in shaping policies that promote economic empowerment and access to education, and their commitment to these issues is vital for the region's development.

Chapter 5: The Rise of Populism in Latin America

Populist Leaders and their Political Strategies

In recent years, Latin America has witnessed the rise of populist leaders who have employed unique political strategies to gain power and shape the region's political landscape. This subchapter explores the characteristics of these leaders and their strategies, aiming to provide diplomats and politicians with a comprehensive understanding of the phenomenon.

Populist leaders in Latin America have capitalized on the dissatisfaction of the masses with traditional politics and institutions. They have successfully tapped into the frustrations of marginalized groups, promising to address their concerns and champion their interests. These leaders often present themselves as the voice of the people, positioning themselves as the ultimate saviors of their nations.

One of the key strategies employed by these populist leaders is the use of charismatic rhetoric and emotional appeal. They master the art of connecting with their audiences on an emotional level, speaking directly to their fears, aspirations, and hopes. By invoking powerful nationalist sentiments and promising radical change, they create a sense of unity and belonging among their supporters.

Another common strategy is the implementation of policies that prioritize the redistribution of wealth and resources. Populist leaders often advocate for social welfare programs, income redistribution, and increased government intervention in the economy. This approach resonates with the masses, particularly those who have been historically marginalized and excluded from the benefits of economic growth.

Furthermore, populist leaders actively engage with social movements and grassroots organizations. They recognize the power of collective action and harness the energy of these movements to amplify their political agenda. By aligning themselves with social causes such as indigenous rights, gender equality, and environmental sustainability, they gain support from diverse sectors of society.

However, it is important to note that the rise of populist leaders in Latin America has not been without controversy. Critics argue that their strategies often undermine democratic institutions and concentrate power in the hands of a few. Furthermore, their economic policies can be unsustainable and lead to long-term negative consequences for the region's economies.

In conclusion, the rise of populist leaders in Latin America has reshaped the political landscape of the region. By understanding their strategies and tactics, diplomats and politicians can better navigate the challenges and opportunities presented by this phenomenon. It is crucial to strike a balance between addressing the legitimate concerns of marginalized groups and safeguarding democratic institutions and long-term economic stability.

Charismatic leadership and mass mobilization

In the last half century, Latin America has witnessed numerous political, social, and economic changes that have shaped the region's trajectory. One significant aspect that has played a pivotal role in these transformations is charismatic leadership and mass mobilization.

Charismatic leadership refers to individuals who possess exceptional personality traits, communication skills, and the ability to inspire and mobilize large groups of people towards a common goal. In Latin America, charismatic leaders have emerged as influential figures, leading mass movements and mobilizing citizens for various causes.

These charismatic leaders have often been at the forefront of political transitions and democratization processes in the region. They have played a crucial role in challenging authoritarian regimes, advocating for human rights, and pushing for greater political participation and representation. Through their charisma and persuasive abilities, they have been able to rally diverse groups and forge strong alliances, ultimately leading to significant political changes.

Mass mobilization, on the other hand, refers to the collective action of large numbers of people who come together to demand social, political, or economic change. Latin America has witnessed numerous social movements over the past decades, addressing issues such as indigenous rights, gender equality, environmental challenges, and more.

Charismatic leaders have often been instrumental in mobilizing these social movements, providing a strong voice and direction to their demands. Through their ability to connect with people, they have been able to galvanize support, raise awareness, and mobilize individuals to take action. These mass mobilizations have played a critical role in shaping Latin American societies, leading to policy changes, recognition of indigenous rights, advancements in gender equality, and increased focus on environmental sustainability.

However, the rise of populism in Latin America has also been closely linked to charismatic leadership and mass mobilization. Populist leaders, often charismatic figures, have tapped into the frustrations and grievances of marginalized groups, promising radical change and challenging the established political and economic order. While charismatic leaders can bring about positive change, they can also exploit the trust and support of the masses for personal gain or pursue policies that are not in the long-term interest of the region.

In conclusion, charismatic leadership and mass mobilization have played a significant role in shaping the political, social, and economic changes in Latin America over the last half century. Charismatic leaders have been at the forefront of political transitions, advocating for human rights, and mobilizing social movements. However, while these leaders can bring about positive change, the rise of populist leaders also highlights the need for critical analysis and scrutiny of their motives and policy agendas. Understanding the impact of charismatic leadership and mass mobilization is crucial for diplomats and politicians as they navigate the complexities of Latin American politics and work towards sustainable progress in the region.

Economic policies and redistribution of wealth

In the last half century, Latin America has witnessed significant political, social, and economic changes. One crucial aspect of these transformations has been the implementation of different economic policies and their impact on the redistribution of wealth in the region. This subchapter aims to provide an in-depth analysis of the diverse approaches and outcomes of economic policies in Latin America.

The impact of neoliberal economic policies on Latin American economies has been a subject of debate among scholars, policymakers, and economists. Neoliberalism, characterized by free trade, deregulation, and privatization, was widely adopted in the region during the 1980s and 1990s. Proponents argued that these policies would stimulate economic growth and development. However, critics have pointed out that neoliberal reforms often resulted in increased inequality and the concentration of wealth in the hands of a few.

Political transitions and democratization processes in Latin America have also played a significant role in shaping economic policies and the redistribution of wealth. As countries transitioned from authoritarian regimes to democracies, new governments faced the challenge of addressing social inequalities and poverty. Some countries implemented progressive tax policies and social programs to reduce poverty and improve access to education and healthcare. Others opted for more market-oriented strategies, emphasizing the role of the private sector in creating economic opportunities.

Social movements have played a crucial role in advocating for more inclusive economic policies and challenging the concentration of wealth in Latin America. Indigenous rights movements, women's empowerment movements, and environmental activists have pushed for policies that prioritize social justice, gender equality, and sustainability.

The rise of populism in Latin America has also influenced economic policies and the redistribution of wealth. Populist leaders, often charismatic and appealing to the masses, have implemented policies aimed at reducing inequality and promoting social welfare. However, the long-term sustainability of these policies has been contested, with some arguing that they can lead to economic instability and a concentration of power.

The effects of foreign intervention on Latin American politics and economies cannot be overlooked. Historically, external powers have influenced economic policies in the region, often prioritizing their own interests. This has sometimes led to the exacerbation of social inequalities and the exploitation of natural resources.

In recent years, there has been a growing recognition of indigenous rights in Latin American countries. Governments have implemented policies aimed at protecting the rights and cultures of indigenous communities, as well as promoting their economic inclusion.

Gender equality and women's empowerment have also gained attention in the region. Efforts have been made to address gender disparities in the labor market, promote women's access to education and healthcare, and combat gender-based violence.

Environmental challenges and sustainability have emerged as critical issues in Latin America. Governments and civil society organizations are increasingly focused on promoting sustainable development, preserving biodiversity, and mitigating the impacts of climate change.

International organizations have played a significant role in shaping economic policies in Latin America. Institutions such as the World Bank, the International Monetary Fund, and regional development banks have provided financial assistance and policy advice to countries in the region.

Finally, globalization has had a profound impact on Latin American economies and cultures. Global trade, foreign direct investment, and the integration of regional markets have opened up new opportunities for economic growth but have also exposed countries to economic volatility and external shocks.

In conclusion, understanding the economic policies implemented in Latin America and their impact on the redistribution of wealth is crucial for diplomats and politicians. This subchapter has provided an overview of the diverse approaches to economic policies in the region, as well as the role of social movements, foreign intervention, indigenous rights, gender equality, environmental sustainability, international organizations, and globalization in shaping the economic landscape of Latin America. By examining these factors, policymakers can make informed decisions to promote inclusive and sustainable economic development in the region.

Challenges to democratic institutions and checks and balances

In the dynamic landscape of Latin America, the journey towards progress has not been without its fair share of challenges. This subchapter delves into the obstacles faced by democratic institutions and the crucial checks and balances that play a vital role in shaping the region's political, social, and economic changes over the last half-century.

One of the primary challenges faced by democratic institutions in Latin America is the fragility of their foundations. Historically, the region has witnessed frequent political transitions and democratization processes, often accompanied by political instability and weak institutions. These transitions, while essential for progress, have posed significant challenges in ensuring the continuity and effectiveness of democratic governance.

Furthermore, the rise of populism in Latin America has also posed challenges to democratic institutions. Populist leaders, with their charismatic appeal and promises of change, have often sought to concentrate power in their hands, eroding the checks and balances that are essential for a healthy democracy. This has led to concerns regarding the erosion of democratic norms, media freedom, and the independence of the judiciary.

Moreover, the effects of foreign intervention on Latin American politics and economies have also challenged democratic institutions. Historically, external intervention by global powers has often undermined democratic processes, supporting authoritarian regimes or interfering in domestic affairs. This interference has often led to political instability and hindered the consolidation of democratic institutions.

Another significant challenge to democratic institutions in Latin America is the recognition and protection of indigenous rights. Despite progress in recent decades, many indigenous communities continue to face discrimination and marginalization, undermining their political representation and participation. Ensuring the recognition and inclusion of indigenous rights within democratic systems remains a critical challenge.

Gender equality and women's empowerment have also been areas of concern for democratic institutions in the region. Despite advancements, women continue to face significant barriers in political representation and decision-making processes. Overcoming these challenges requires not only legal and institutional changes but also a shift in societal attitudes towards gender equality.

Furthermore, environmental challenges and sustainability have emerged as critical issues for democratic institutions. Latin America's rich biodiversity and natural resources face threats from unsustainable development practices, deforestation, and climate change. Ensuring effective environmental governance and sustainable policies is crucial for the long-term well-being of the region and its people.

In conclusion, the path to progress in Latin America has been marked by various challenges to democratic institutions and checks and balances. From political transitions and populism to foreign intervention and environmental sustainability, these challenges require concerted efforts from diplomats and politicians in addressing the underlying issues and strengthening democratic governance. Only through the recognition and protection of indigenous rights, gender equality, and sustainable policies can Latin America overcome these obstacles and continue its journey towards progress.

Chapter 6: The Effects of Foreign Intervention on Latin American Politics and Economies

Historical Context of Foreign Intervention

The Historical Context of Foreign Intervention in Latin America

Latin America's Path to Progress: Political, Social, and Economic Changes in the Last Half Century

Introduction

In understanding the political, social, and economic changes that have shaped Latin America over the past half-century, it is essential to examine the historical context of foreign intervention. Diplomats and politicians must grasp the impact of external forces on the region's development to effectively navigate its complexities. This subchapter delves into the historical backdrop of foreign intervention in Latin America, shedding light on its implications for the continent's political and economic trajectories.

Colonial Legacy and Independence Movements

Latin America's historical context is rooted in its colonial past, with European powers dominating the region for centuries. The struggle for independence in the 19th century marked a turning point, as Latin American countries sought to break free from foreign control and establish their own political identities. However, the legacy of colonialism continued to shape the region's social and economic structures, often leaving it vulnerable to foreign influence.

The Cold War and Geopolitical Power Struggles

The Cold War era witnessed heightened foreign intervention in Latin America, as global powers sought to expand their spheres of influence. The United States and the Soviet Union engaged in a geopolitical struggle, leading to interventions in countries like Cuba, Nicaragua, and Chile. These interventions often fueled political instability and social unrest, shaping the region's political transitions and democratization processes.

Neoliberal Economic Policies and Structural Adjustment Programs

During the late 20th century, Latin America experienced a shift towards neoliberal economic policies, influenced by international financial institutions like the International Monetary Fund and the World Bank. These policies emphasized free-market principles, privatization, and deregulation. However, their implementation often resulted in economic crises, exacerbating social inequalities and leading to protests and social movements.

The Rise of Populism and Anti-Imperialist Movements

In response to the negative consequences of neoliberal policies and foreign intervention, Latin America witnessed the rise of populism and anti-imperialist movements. Leaders like Hugo Chávez in Venezuela and Evo Morales in Bolivia challenged traditional power structures, advocating for greater autonomy and social justice. These movements reshaped Latin American societies, amplifying demands for indigenous rights, gender equality, and environmental sustainability.

Conclusion

Understanding the historical context of foreign intervention in Latin America is crucial for diplomats and politicians seeking to address the region's political, social, and economic challenges. From the colonial legacy to the Cold War era and the rise of populism, external forces have shaped Latin American development in profound ways. By acknowledging and addressing the effects of foreign intervention, stakeholders can work towards a more equitable and sustainable path to progress in the region.

United States interventions during the Cold War

Subchapter: United States Interventions during the Cold War

Introduction:

United States interventions during the Cold War in Latin America played a significant role in shaping the political, social, and economic landscape of the region. This subchapter aims to provide diplomats and politicians with an in-depth understanding of the various interventions carried out by the United States and their lasting impacts on Latin American countries.

Historical Context:

The Cold War era witnessed a struggle between the United States and the Soviet Union for global influence. Latin America became a battleground for ideological competition, leading to a series of interventions by the United States. These interventions were often justified as efforts to safeguard democracy and prevent the spread of communism.

Political Interventions:

The United States supported and often orchestrated the overthrow of democratically elected governments in Latin America, replacing them with military regimes favorable to American interests. Examples include the overthrow of Guatemala's President Jacobo Arbenz in 1954 and Chile's President Salvador Allende in 1973. These interventions contributed to political instability and undermined the region's democratic processes.

Economic Interventions:

The United States implemented neoliberal economic policies in Latin America during the Cold War, promoting free-market capitalism and privatization. These policies, often imposed through conditional loans from international financial institutions, led to the dismantling of local industries, exacerbating income inequality and poverty. Latin American economies became heavily dependent on exports, leaving them vulnerable to global economic fluctuations.

Social Impacts:

US interventions during the Cold War had profound social consequences in Latin America. Social movements emerged as a response to repressive military regimes, demanding social justice, human rights, and democratic reforms. These movements played a pivotal role in shaping Latin American societies and challenging existing power structures.

Legacy and Lessons Learned:

The long-term effects of US interventions are still felt in Latin America today. They have contributed to a legacy of political instability, economic inequality, and social unrest. Understanding this history is crucial for diplomats and politicians to develop policies that promote stability, inclusivity, and sustainable development in the region.

Conclusion:

The United States interventions during the Cold War in Latin America had far-reaching consequences that continue to shape the political, social, and economic realities of the region. By reflecting on the past, diplomats and politicians can work towards building a more equitable and prosperous future for Latin America, free from foreign intervention and guided by the principles of democracy and self-determination.

Influence of international organizations and multinational corporations

International organizations and multinational corporations have played a significant role in shaping the political, social, and economic changes in Latin America over the last half century. Their influence has been both positive and negative, and their actions have had a profound impact on the region.

From an economic perspective, multinational corporations have brought investment, technology, and employment opportunities to Latin American countries. These corporations have introduced new industries, expanded trade, and stimulated economic growth. However, their presence has also led to the exploitation of natural resources, labor abuses, and environmental degradation. The influence of multinational corporations on Latin American economies has often been characterized by a tension between economic development and social and environmental sustainability.

International organizations, on the other hand, have played a crucial role in shaping policies and promoting cooperation among Latin American countries. Organizations such as the United Nations, the World Bank, and the International Monetary Fund have provided financial assistance, technical expertise, and policy advice to governments in the region. They have supported initiatives aimed at poverty reduction, education, healthcare, and infrastructure development. However, the influence of these organizations has not always been welcomed by all Latin American countries, as they have been accused of promoting neoliberal economic policies that prioritize market-oriented reforms over social welfare.

The influence of international organizations and multinational corporations has also had political implications. Their involvement in Latin American politics has been seen as a form of foreign intervention, with some countries perceiving it as a threat to their sovereignty. However, these organizations have also played a role in supporting political transitions and democratization processes in the region. They have advocated for human rights, the rule of law, and democratic governance, and have provided technical assistance for electoral processes and institutional reforms.

In conclusion, the influence of international organizations and multinational corporations in Latin America has been significant and complex. Their actions have impacted the political, social, and economic changes in the region, shaping policies, promoting development, and sometimes creating tensions. As diplomats and politicians, it is important to understand and carefully navigate the influence of these actors to ensure the progress and well-being of Latin American countries.

Shift in foreign policy approaches towards Latin America

Over the past half century, Latin America has witnessed a significant shift in foreign policy approaches from global powers. This subchapter examines the changing dynamics of international relations with Latin America, focusing on the evolving strategies, interests, and priorities of various countries.

Diplomats and politicians, as key stakeholders in international relations, need to be aware of these shifts to effectively navigate the complex landscape of Latin American politics, social issues, and economic changes. Understanding the historical context and current trends will enable them to make informed decisions and forge beneficial relationships with Latin American countries.

The traditional approach of foreign powers towards Latin America was often characterized by interventionism, with a focus on securing economic and political advantages. However, in recent decades, there has been a noticeable shift towards a more cooperative and mutually beneficial engagement. This change can be attributed to several factors.

Firstly, the impact of neoliberal economic policies on Latin American economies has played a crucial role. Many countries in the region experienced economic crises, prompting a reevaluation of their economic models. This led to a new wave of reforms, including the opening up of markets and attracting foreign investment. As a result, foreign powers began to view Latin America as an attractive destination for trade and investment, leading to a shift in their foreign policy approaches.

Furthermore, political transitions and democratization processes in Latin America have contributed to this shift. The region has witnessed a significant increase in democratic governance, with more governments being elected through free and fair elections. This has led to a greater emphasis on dialogue and cooperation, as foreign powers seek to engage with these newly democratic nations.

Social movements have also played a pivotal role in shaping foreign policy approaches towards Latin America. The rise of populist movements and their demands for social justice, equality, and indigenous rights have garnered international attention. Foreign powers have recognized the importance of supporting these movements and addressing their demands, leading to a change in their foreign policy priorities.

Moreover, the recognition of indigenous rights and the promotion of gender equality and women's empowerment have become key issues in Latin American countries. Foreign powers have increasingly focused on supporting these causes and incorporating them into their foreign policy agendas.

Environmental challenges and sustainability in Latin America have also influenced foreign policy approaches. The region's rich biodiversity and natural resources have attracted global attention, leading to increased cooperation in areas such as climate change mitigation, conservation, and sustainable development.

In conclusion, the shift in foreign policy approaches towards Latin America has been driven by a combination of economic, political, social, and environmental factors. As diplomats and politicians, understanding these shifts is essential for effective engagement with the region. By acknowledging the changing dynamics and aligning their strategies with the evolving priorities of Latin American countries, foreign powers can foster mutually beneficial relationships and contribute to the progress and development of the region.

Chapter 7: Indigenous Rights and their Recognition in Latin American Countries

International Framework for Indigenous Rights

In the last half-century, Latin America has witnessed significant political, social, and economic changes. One crucial aspect of these changes is the recognition and protection of indigenous rights. The international framework for indigenous rights has played a significant role in shaping the policies and attitudes towards indigenous communities in Latin America.

Indigenous peoples in Latin America have historically suffered from discrimination, marginalization, and the violation of their rights. However, with the emergence of global human rights norms and the strengthening of international institutions, there has been a growing recognition of the importance of indigenous rights.

The United Nations Declaration on the Rights of Indigenous Peoples (UNDRIP), adopted in 2007, is a critical milestone in the international framework for indigenous rights. The declaration recognizes the collective rights of indigenous peoples, including their rights to land, self-determination, cultural preservation, and participation in decision-making processes. It also emphasizes the need to address historical injustices and ensure the full participation of indigenous peoples in all aspects of society.

Latin American countries have made significant progress in recognizing indigenous rights and integrating them into their legal and political systems. Many countries have enacted legislation that explicitly recognizes the rights of indigenous peoples and establishes mechanisms for their participation in decision-making processes. For example, Bolivia, Ecuador, and Colombia have constitutional provisions that recognize the rights of indigenous peoples and guarantee their representation in national institutions.

However, despite these advancements, challenges persist in the implementation of indigenous rights. Many indigenous communities continue to face discrimination, poverty, and limited access to basic services such as healthcare and education. Land conflicts and natural resource extraction also pose significant challenges to indigenous rights, as they often result in the displacement and marginalization of indigenous communities.

Diplomats and politicians play a crucial role in advancing the recognition and protection of indigenous rights in Latin America. They can promote dialogue and cooperation between governments, indigenous communities, and civil society organizations to address the challenges faced by indigenous peoples. They can also advocate for the implementation of international norms and the strengthening of legal frameworks to ensure the full realization of indigenous rights.

In conclusion, the international framework for indigenous rights has played a pivotal role in shaping the recognition and protection of indigenous rights in Latin America. While progress has been made, challenges persist, and further efforts are needed to ensure the full inclusion and empowerment of indigenous communities. Diplomats and politicians have a crucial role in advancing this agenda and creating a more inclusive and equitable society in Latin America.

United Nations Declaration on the Rights of Indigenous Peoples

The United Nations Declaration on the Rights of Indigenous Peoples is a landmark document that addresses the historical marginalization and discrimination faced by indigenous communities in Latin America and around the world. This subchapter will explore the significance of this declaration in the context of Latin America's political, social, and economic changes over the last half century.

Latin America has a rich and diverse indigenous population, with over 400 different indigenous groups spread across the region. These communities have long been subjected to human rights abuses, land dispossession, and cultural erasure. However, in recent decades, there has been a growing recognition of the importance of indigenous rights and the need for their protection and preservation.

The United Nations Declaration on the Rights of Indigenous Peoples was adopted by the UN General Assembly in 2007 and provides a comprehensive framework for the promotion and protection of indigenous rights. It recognizes the right to self-determination, the right to land and resources, the right to cultural identity, and the right to participate in decision-making processes that affect indigenous communities.

In Latin America, the declaration has had a profound impact on indigenous rights. Many countries in the region have taken steps to incorporate the principles of the declaration into their national legislation and policies. This includes recognizing indigenous land rights, promoting bilingual education, and ensuring indigenous participation in political processes.

The declaration has also been instrumental in empowering indigenous communities and fostering social change. Indigenous movements and social organizations have used the declaration to advocate for their rights and to challenge discriminatory practices. They have been able to mobilize support both domestically and internationally, leading to greater awareness and action on indigenous issues.

Furthermore, the declaration has contributed to the broader political transitions and democratization processes in Latin America. It has highlighted the importance of inclusivity and diversity in creating more equitable and just societies. By recognizing the rights of indigenous peoples, governments have been forced to confront historical injustices and work towards reconciliation and social cohesion.

In conclusion, the United Nations Declaration on the Rights of Indigenous Peoples has played a crucial role in shaping the political, social, and economic changes in Latin America over the last half century. It has been instrumental in recognizing and protecting indigenous rights, empowering indigenous communities, and fostering social change. As diplomats and politicians, it is vital to continue supporting the implementation of the declaration and working towards a more inclusive and just society for all.

Inter-American Court of Human Rights and indigenous land rights

The Inter-American Court of Human Rights (IACHR) plays a crucial role in protecting and promoting human rights in Latin America. One significant area of focus for the court is indigenous land rights, which have been a long-standing issue in the region. This subchapter will explore the IACHR's efforts to address indigenous land rights and the impact it has had on Latin American societies.

Indigenous land rights are a fundamental aspect of indigenous cultures and their existence. However, throughout history, indigenous communities in Latin America have faced significant challenges in asserting and defending their land rights. The colonization process, followed by the expansion of modern nation-states, often resulted in the dispossession and marginalization of indigenous peoples from their ancestral lands.

Recognizing the importance of indigenous land rights and the need to address historical injustices, the IACHR has taken significant steps to protect and promote these rights. The court has developed a jurisprudence that recognizes indigenous peoples' rights to their ancestral lands and the importance of their cultural and spiritual connection to those lands. It has also emphasized the need for states to obtain the free, prior, and informed consent of indigenous communities before undertaking any development projects on their lands.

The IACHR's rulings on indigenous land rights have had a profound impact on Latin American societies. They have set important precedents for national courts and governments, encouraging them to recognize and respect the rights of indigenous peoples. As a result, several Latin American countries have implemented legal and policy reforms to better protect indigenous land rights. These reforms have included the demarcation and titling of indigenous territories, the establishment of consultation mechanisms, and the recognition of indigenous customary law.

Moreover, the IACHR's work on indigenous land rights has also sparked important social movements and activism across the region. Indigenous communities, supported by civil society organizations, have mobilized to demand the recognition and respect of their land rights. Their efforts have led to increased awareness and understanding of indigenous issues and have contributed to broader societal changes in Latin America.

In conclusion, the Inter-American Court of Human Rights has played a vital role in advocating for indigenous land rights in Latin America. Its efforts have had a significant impact, both legally and socially, by promoting the recognition and respect of indigenous land rights and fostering broader societal changes. However, despite these advancements, challenges remain, and continued efforts are needed to ensure the full realization of indigenous land rights in the region.

Chapter 8: Gender Equality and Women's Empowerment in Latin America

Legal and Policy Reforms for Gender Equality

Introduction

In the last half century, Latin America has experienced significant political, social, and economic changes. These changes have shaped the region, impacting various aspects of life, including gender equality and women's empowerment. This subchapter explores the legal and policy reforms that have been implemented to promote gender equality in Latin America. It highlights the progress made, challenges faced, and the role of diplomats and politicians in driving these reforms.

The Need for Reforms

Latin America has long been characterized by gender inequalities, with women facing discrimination and limited opportunities. Recognizing the importance of gender equality for social progress and economic development, governments, international organizations, and civil society have pushed for legal and policy reforms to address these disparities.

Legal Reforms

Several countries in Latin America have enacted legislation aimed at promoting gender equality. These reforms include laws against gender-based violence, equal pay for equal work, and quotas to increase women's representation in politics and decision-making positions. Diplomats and politicians have played a crucial role in advocating for and implementing these legal reforms, both domestically and internationally.

Policy Reforms

In addition to legal changes, policy reforms have been implemented to promote gender equality in Latin America. Governments have developed national action plans, strategies, and programs that focus on women's empowerment, access to education and healthcare, and economic opportunities. These policies aim to address the structural barriers that prevent women from fully participating in society and the economy.

Challenges and Opportunities

While progress has been made, challenges remain in achieving gender equality in Latin America. Deep-rooted cultural norms, gender stereotypes, and limited resources hinder the full implementation of legal and policy reforms. Diplomats and politicians must continue to advocate for gender equality, address these challenges, and seize opportunities to further advance women's rights.

Conclusion

Legal and policy reforms have played a vital role in promoting gender equality in Latin America over the last half century. Diplomats and politicians have been at the forefront of these efforts, championing change and driving progress. However, there is still much work to be done to overcome the remaining challenges and ensure that women in Latin America have equal opportunities and rights. By continuing to prioritize gender equality, policymakers can contribute to the region's overall progress and foster a more inclusive and equitable society.

Gender-based violence legislation

Gender-based violence legislation refers to the laws and regulations enacted by Latin American countries to address and combat violence against women and other gender-based crimes. Over the last half century, there have been significant political, social, and economic changes in Latin America, and the issue of gender-based violence has emerged as a critical concern. This subchapter examines the legislative measures taken by countries in the region to tackle this pervasive problem.

In recent years, Latin America has witnessed a growing recognition of the importance of combating gender-based violence and promoting gender equality. Governments and civil society organizations have been working together to develop comprehensive legislation that not only criminalizes violence against women but also addresses the underlying causes and provides support to survivors.

Several countries in the region have passed laws that specifically target gender-based violence. These laws define various forms of violence, such as domestic violence, sexual harassment, and femicide, and outline the legal consequences for perpetrators. They also establish mechanisms for reporting incidents, providing support services to survivors, and raising awareness about the issue.

One notable example is the "Ley Modelo" (Model Law) on Violence Against Women, which has been adopted by several countries in Latin America. This law provides a comprehensive framework for addressing gender-based violence and includes provisions for prevention, protection, punishment, and reparation. It also recognizes the rights of survivors and ensures their access to justice and support services.

However, despite these legislative advancements, challenges remain in implementing and enforcing gender-based violence legislation. Limited resources, inadequate training for law enforcement officials, and cultural norms that perpetuate gender inequality hinder progress in this area. It is essential for diplomats and politicians to collaborate with international organizations, civil society groups, and the private sector to overcome these obstacles and ensure effective implementation of gender-based violence legislation.

In conclusion, gender-based violence legislation has become a critical component of Latin America's path to progress. By addressing this issue, countries can promote gender equality, protect women's rights, and create safer and more inclusive societies. However, ongoing efforts are needed to strengthen the implementation and enforcement of these laws and to challenge the social norms that perpetuate gender-based violence. Diplomats and politicians have a crucial role to play in supporting these efforts and ensuring that gender equality and women's empowerment remain at the top of the political agenda in Latin America.

Maternal and reproductive health rights

Maternal and reproductive health rights play a crucial role in shaping the political, social, and economic changes in Latin America over the last half century. This subchapter aims to address the importance of these rights, their impact on the region, and the challenges that still exist in achieving gender equality and women's empowerment.

Throughout Latin America, the recognition and protection of maternal and reproductive health rights have become vital components of the political agenda. These rights encompass a broad range of issues, including access to healthcare services, family planning, safe and legal abortion, and comprehensive sexuality education. By promoting and ensuring these rights, governments can improve the overall well-being of their citizens and contribute to sustainable development.

In recent decades, significant progress has been made in advancing maternal and reproductive health rights in Latin America. Governments have implemented policies and programs to expand access to sexual and reproductive healthcare services, reduce maternal mortality rates, and empower women to make informed decisions about their bodies and reproductive choices. Moreover, international organizations and NGOs have played a crucial role in advocating for these rights and providing technical assistance to governments in implementing effective policies.

However, despite these advancements, challenges persist. In many Latin American countries, particularly in rural and indigenous communities, access to quality maternal and reproductive healthcare remains limited. Women face barriers such as cultural norms, lack of education, and restrictive legislation that hinder their ability to exercise their reproductive rights. Furthermore, the region still grapples with high rates of teenage pregnancy, unsafe abortions, and gender-based violence, highlighting the need for continued efforts to address these issues comprehensively.

To achieve gender equality and women's empowerment, it is crucial for diplomats and politicians to prioritize maternal and reproductive health rights in their policy agendas. This includes allocating adequate resources to healthcare systems, promoting comprehensive sexuality education, decriminalizing abortion, and ensuring the provision of safe and affordable contraception. Additionally, governments must address the underlying social and cultural norms that perpetuate gender inequality, prioritizing the inclusion and participation of women in decision-making processes.

In conclusion, maternal and reproductive health rights have emerged as key factors in the political, social, and economic changes in Latin America over the last half century. While progress has been made, there is still work to be done to ensure equal access to healthcare services and empower women to make informed decisions about their reproductive health. By prioritizing these rights, diplomats and politicians can contribute to the overall development and well-being of the region, and advance gender equality and women's empowerment in Latin America.

Representation of women in politics and decision-making

In recent decades, Latin America has witnessed significant progress in the representation of women in politics and decision-making processes. This subchapter explores the strides made by the region towards achieving gender equality and women's empowerment, and the challenges that still lie ahead.

Latin America has made remarkable progress in increasing the number of women in political positions. Several countries have implemented gender quotas or affirmative action policies to ensure women's participation in decision-making bodies. These measures have resulted in a significant rise in the number of women legislators, ministers, and even presidents. For instance, Brazil, Argentina, and Chile have all elected female presidents in the past decade.

Despite these advancements, women still face numerous barriers when it comes to political participation. Deep-rooted gender stereotypes and cultural norms often limit women's access to political leadership positions. Additionally, women frequently encounter discrimination and gender-based violence in the political arena, which can deter their involvement. Overcoming these challenges requires not only legal reforms but also changes in societal attitudes towards gender roles and women's rights.

The benefits of increased women's representation in politics are manifold. Research consistently shows that diverse decision-making bodies lead to better governance and more inclusive policies. Women in politics often prioritize issues such as healthcare, education, and social welfare, which are crucial for the advancement of society as a whole. Furthermore, women's participation in politics can serve as a powerful symbol of empowerment for other women, inspiring them to engage in civic and political life.

To further promote gender equality in politics, it is essential to address the underrepresentation of women from marginalized groups, such as indigenous women and Afro-Latinas. These women face intersecting forms of discrimination and often experience multiple barriers to political participation. Policies and initiatives must be implemented to ensure their inclusion and to amplify their voices in decision-making processes.

In conclusion, while Latin America has made significant progress in the representation of women in politics and decision-making, there is still much work to be done. Achieving true gender equality requires not only increasing the number of women in political positions but also challenging societal norms and addressing intersecting forms of discrimination. By fostering inclusive and diverse political systems, Latin America can continue on its path towards progress and equality.

Chapter 9: Environmental Challenges and Sustainability in Latin America

Deforestation and Biodiversity Conservation

Introduction:

Latin America is home to some of the most diverse and fragile ecosystems in the world. However, over the last half century, the region has faced significant challenges in preserving its biodiversity due to widespread deforestation. This subchapter aims to shed light on the importance of biodiversity conservation and the efforts made by Latin American countries to address the issue.

Deforestation and its Impact on Biodiversity:

Deforestation has been a major environmental concern in Latin America, fueled by factors such as agricultural expansion, logging, and infrastructure development. As a result, numerous species have been pushed to the brink of extinction, and delicate ecosystems have been irreversibly damaged. This loss of biodiversity not only threatens the region's natural heritage but also has severe consequences for human livelihoods, including the disruption of ecosystem services such as clean water, climate regulation, and food security.

Efforts in Biodiversity Conservation:

Recognizing the urgency of the situation, Latin American countries have taken significant steps to conserve their biodiversity. Governments have established protected areas, national parks, and biosphere reserves to safeguard critical habitats. Additionally, international collaborations and partnerships with non-governmental organizations have facilitated the implementation of conservation programs and initiatives.

Challenges and Solutions:

Despite the progress made, challenges persist. Weak governance, corruption, and limited resources hinder effective conservation efforts. Moreover, the pressure to meet economic development goals often conflicts with environmental concerns. However, innovative approaches such as sustainable land management, community-based conservation, and the integration of traditional knowledge have shown promising results in reconciling economic growth with biodiversity conservation.

The Role of Diplomats and Politicians:

Diplomats and politicians play a crucial role in addressing the issue of deforestation and biodiversity conservation in Latin America. Through international agreements, such as the United Nations Framework Convention on Climate Change and the Convention on Biological Diversity, they can advocate for stronger environmental regulations, promote sustainable practices, and secure financial support for conservation initiatives.

Conclusion:

Deforestation poses a significant threat to Latin America's rich biodiversity, impacting both the environment and human well-being. Nevertheless, with concerted efforts from governments, international organizations, and the active engagement of diplomats and politicians, there is hope for reversing the trend of deforestation and ensuring the long-term sustainability of Latin America's natural heritage. By prioritizing biodiversity conservation, the region can pave the way for a more sustainable and prosperous future for its people and ecosystems.

Extractive industries and indigenous lands

Extractive industries, such as mining, oil, and gas, have long been a contentious issue in Latin America, particularly when it comes to their impact on indigenous lands. This subchapter explores the complex relationship between extractive industries and indigenous communities, shedding light on the political, social, and economic changes that have taken place in the region over the last half century.

Latin America has a rich history of indigenous cultures and traditions, many of which are deeply connected to their ancestral lands. However, these lands often contain valuable natural resources that attract the attention of extractive industries. This has led to conflicts and tensions between indigenous communities and governments, as well as multinational corporations seeking to exploit these resources.

One of the key challenges in this context has been the recognition and protection of indigenous rights. Over the last half century, there has been a growing recognition of indigenous peoples' rights in many Latin American countries. This has been accompanied by legal reforms and the establishment of mechanisms to ensure indigenous participation in decision-making processes related to extractive industries.

However, implementation has often fallen short, with indigenous communities continuing to face displacement, environmental degradation, and human rights abuses. This has sparked social movements and protests, as indigenous peoples have increasingly organized to defend their lands and assert their rights.

The impact of neoliberal economic policies on Latin American economies has played a significant role in shaping the dynamics of extractive industries and indigenous lands. The liberalization of markets and the promotion of foreign investment have often prioritized economic growth over social and environmental concerns. This has disproportionately affected indigenous communities, who have historically been marginalized and excluded from the benefits of development.

Political transitions and democratization processes in Latin America have also had an impact on the recognition of indigenous rights. As countries transitioned from authoritarian regimes to democracies, indigenous movements gained greater visibility and political power. This has allowed for the inclusion of indigenous perspectives in policy-making processes and the adoption of more inclusive approaches to natural resource management.

In recent years, there has been a growing awareness of the importance of sustainable development and the need to balance economic growth with social and environmental considerations. This has led to the emergence of initiatives that seek to promote responsible extractive industries and ensure the protection of indigenous lands.

International organizations, such as the United Nations and the Inter-American Commission on Human Rights, have played a crucial role in advocating for indigenous rights and supporting efforts to ensure their recognition and protection. However, challenges persist, and there is still much work to be done to address the power imbalances and inequalities that continue to shape the relationship between extractive industries and indigenous lands in Latin America.

In conclusion, the relationship between extractive industries and indigenous lands in Latin America is complex and multifaceted. It is shaped by political, social, and economic changes that have taken place in the region over the last half century. While progress has been made in recognizing and protecting indigenous rights, challenges remain, and further efforts are needed to ensure the sustainable and equitable management of natural resources. Diplomats and politicians have a crucial role to play in promoting dialogue, fostering inclusive policies, and supporting the empowerment of indigenous communities in order to achieve a more just and sustainable future for all in Latin America.

Conservation policies and protected areas

Conservation policies and protected areas have played a crucial role in Latin America's path to progress over the last half century. As diplomats and politicians, it is important to understand the significance of these policies and their impact on the political, social, and economic changes in the region.

Latin America is home to some of the world's most biodiverse ecosystems, including the Amazon rainforest, the Galapagos Islands, and the Patagonian steppe. Recognizing the value of these natural resources, many countries in the region have implemented conservation policies and established protected areas to safeguard their unique flora and fauna.

These conservation policies have not only helped preserve biodiversity but also contributed to sustainable economic development. Protected areas have become important tourist destinations, attracting visitors from around the world and generating revenue for local communities. Additionally, these areas provide ecosystem services such as water regulation, carbon sequestration, and soil fertility, which are vital for agricultural productivity and climate change mitigation.

However, the implementation of conservation policies has not been without challenges. The expansion of agriculture, mining, and infrastructure projects has led to deforestation, habitat destruction, and pollution in some areas. Balancing economic development with environmental protection requires effective governance, strong institutions, and the involvement of local communities.

In recent years, there has been a growing recognition of the rights of indigenous peoples and their role in conservation efforts. Many Latin

American countries have granted land titles and recognized indigenous territories, empowering these communities to manage their lands sustainably. Indigenous knowledge and practices have proven invaluable in maintaining the balance between human activities and nature.

International organizations have also played a significant role in shaping conservation policies in Latin America. Through funding, technical assistance, and capacity building, these organizations have supported the establishment and management of protected areas. They have also promoted collaborative initiatives between countries, facilitating the exchange of knowledge and best practices.

As we navigate the challenges of the 21st century, it is crucial for diplomats and politicians to prioritize conservation policies and protected areas. Ensuring the sustainability of Latin America's natural resources will not only benefit the region but also contribute to global efforts towards environmental preservation and sustainable development. By working together, we can build a prosperous future that respects the rights of indigenous peoples, promotes gender equality, and safeguards the environment for generations to come.

Chapter 10: The Role of International Organizations in Shaping Latin American Policies

United Nations and Regional Organizations

The United Nations (UN) and regional organizations have played a significant role in shaping the political, social, and economic changes in Latin America over the last half century. As diplomats and politicians, it is crucial to understand the impact these entities have had on the region and how they have influenced various aspects of Latin American societies.

The UN has been a key player in promoting peace, security, and development in Latin America. Through its various specialized agencies, such as the United Nations Development Programme (UNDP) and the United Nations Educational, Scientific and Cultural Organization (UNESCO), the UN has provided technical assistance and financial support to Latin American countries in their efforts to overcome political instability, poverty, and inequality.

Regional organizations such as the Organization of American States (OAS) and the Union of South American Nations (UNASUR) have also played a crucial role in promoting regional integration and cooperation. These organizations have facilitated dialogue and cooperation among Latin American countries, leading to the establishment of common policies and initiatives aimed at addressing shared challenges.

The impact of neoliberal economic policies on Latin American economies cannot be ignored. In the last half century, Latin American countries embarked on a path of economic liberalization, opening up their markets to foreign investment and trade. While these policies brought some economic growth and modernization, they also resulted in increased inequality and social unrest. Regional organizations, such as the Economic Commission for Latin America and the Caribbean (ECLAC), have been instrumental in analyzing the consequences of these policies and proposing alternatives to promote more inclusive and sustainable development.

Political transitions and democratization processes have been a defining feature of Latin America in recent decades. Many countries in the region have transitioned from authoritarian regimes to democracies, often with the support and guidance of the UN and regional organizations. These transitions have brought greater political freedoms and increased citizen participation, although challenges remain in consolidating democratic institutions and ensuring respect for human rights.

Social movements have played a crucial role in shaping Latin American societies. From labor movements to indigenous rights movements, these grassroots organizations have fought for social justice, equality, and recognition of marginalized groups. The UN and regional organizations have provided a platform for these movements to voice their concerns and advocate for policy changes.

The rise of populism in Latin America has had both positive and negative consequences. Populist leaders have often promised to address the needs and aspirations of marginalized populations, but their policies have sometimes undermined democratic institutions and created divisions within society. The UN and regional organizations have been instrumental in promoting dialogue and mediating conflicts in these contexts.

Foreign intervention has had a significant impact on Latin American politics and economies. Historically, Latin America has been subject to intervention by external powers, leading to political instability and economic dependency. The UN and regional organizations have been advocates for sovereignty and self-determination, promoting non-intervention and supporting Latin American countries in their efforts to assert their independence.

Recognition of indigenous rights has been a significant development in Latin American countries. The UN and regional organizations have played a crucial role in promoting the rights of indigenous peoples, leading to constitutional reforms and the establishment of mechanisms to protect their cultural heritage and land rights.

Gender equality and women's empowerment have gained momentum in Latin America in recent years. The UN and regional organizations have been vocal advocates for gender mainstreaming and the advancement of women's rights. Efforts to address gender-based violence, promote women's political participation, and ensure equal access to education and employment opportunities are ongoing.

Environmental challenges and sustainability have become pressing issues in Latin America. The region is home to diverse ecosystems and natural resources, but it is also vulnerable to climate change, deforestation, and pollution. The UN and regional organizations have been at the forefront of promoting sustainable development and supporting Latin American countries in their efforts to mitigate environmental degradation.

The role of international organizations, including the UN and regional organizations, in shaping Latin American policies cannot be overstated. These entities have provided technical expertise, financial resources, and a platform for dialogue and cooperation among countries in the region. Their involvement has contributed to the formulation of regional agendas and the implementation of policies aimed at addressing shared challenges.

Globalization has had a profound impact on Latin American economies and cultures. Increased trade and investment flows, technological advancements, and the exchange of ideas and information have transformed societies and economies in the region. The UN and regional organizations have been important actors in ensuring that the benefits of globalization are shared equitably and that the region's cultural diversity is respected and preserved.

In conclusion, the United Nations and regional organizations have played a crucial role in shaping Latin America's political, social, and economic changes over the last half century. As diplomats and politicians, it is essential to understand the impact of these entities on the region and to engage in meaningful dialogue and cooperation to address the challenges and opportunities that lie ahead.

Economic cooperation and trade agreements

Economic cooperation and trade agreements have played a crucial role in shaping Latin America's path to progress over the last half century. As diplomats and politicians, it is essential for us to understand the significance of these agreements and their impact on the political, social, and economic changes in the region.

Latin America has witnessed a significant shift in economic policies during this period, with the rise of neoliberalism. This approach, emphasizing free markets, privatization, and deregulation, has had both positive and negative consequences for Latin American economies. While it has led to increased foreign investment and economic growth in some countries, it has also exacerbated inequalities and social unrest in others.

Political transitions and democratization processes have been another defining feature of Latin America's recent history. Many countries in the region have transitioned from authoritarian regimes to democratic systems, allowing for greater political participation and accountability. These transitions have been accompanied by social movements that have played a critical role in shaping Latin American societies and advocating for the rights of marginalized communities.

The rise of populism in Latin America has also had a significant impact on the region's political landscape. Populist leaders have emerged, promising to address social inequalities and challenge existing power structures. However, their policies have often been divisive and have led to political polarization, undermining democratic institutions and economic stability.

Foreign intervention has long been a contentious issue in Latin American politics and economies. Historical interventions by global powers have had lasting effects on the region, often perpetuating economic dependency and political instability. Recognizing the rights of indigenous communities and promoting gender equality and women's empowerment have become important issues in Latin America. Efforts to address these issues have included legal reforms, affirmative action policies, and the creation of specialized institutions.

Environmental challenges and sustainability have become increasingly important in Latin America. The region is rich in natural resources, but unsustainable practices such as deforestation and resource extraction have led to environmental degradation and threats to biodiversity. International organizations have played a significant role in shaping Latin American policies, providing technical assistance and financial support for development projects.

Finally, the influence of globalization on Latin American economies and cultures cannot be ignored. Globalization has brought both opportunities and challenges, with increased trade and investment, but also increased competition and vulnerability to external shocks. It is essential for diplomats and politicians to understand these dynamics and work towards promoting inclusive and sustainable economic growth in the region.

In conclusion, economic cooperation and trade agreements have been instrumental in shaping Latin America's path to progress. As diplomats and politicians, it is our responsibility to navigate these complex issues and work towards promoting political, social, and economic changes that benefit all segments of society in Latin America.

Human rights monitoring and accountability mechanisms

Human rights monitoring and accountability mechanisms have played a crucial role in shaping the political, social, and economic changes in Latin America over the last half century. This subchapter explores the significance of these mechanisms and their impact on the region's development.

Latin America has witnessed a tumultuous history marked by dictatorships, civil wars, and social unrest. In response to these challenges, human rights monitoring and accountability mechanisms have emerged as essential tools to promote justice, democracy, and respect for fundamental rights.

One of the most notable mechanisms is the Inter-American Commission on Human Rights (IACHR), established in 1959. This organization has been instrumental in investigating human rights violations, providing victims with a platform to seek justice, and holding governments accountable for their actions. Its work has contributed to significant political transitions and democratization processes in the region, helping to dismantle oppressive regimes and promote the rule of law.

Moreover, social movements have played a crucial role in advocating for human rights and shaping Latin American societies. From labor unions fighting for workers' rights to indigenous communities demanding recognition and respect, these movements have been instrumental in challenging oppressive structures and promoting inclusive policies. Human rights monitoring and accountability mechanisms have provided a platform for these movements to voice their concerns and seek redress for past injustices.

The rise of populism in Latin America has also posed challenges to human rights. Some populist leaders have undermined democratic institutions and violated human rights in their pursuit of power. In such instances, human rights monitoring and accountability mechanisms have played a vital role in exposing these abuses and mobilizing international pressure to protect human rights.

Foreign intervention has also had a profound impact on Latin American politics and economies, often leading to human rights violations and socio-economic inequalities. Human rights monitoring and accountability mechanisms have helped shed light on such interventions and hold responsible parties accountable, ensuring that the voice of the people is heard and their rights protected.

Recognizing the rights of indigenous communities and promoting gender equality have been key issues in Latin America. Human rights monitoring and accountability mechanisms have been crucial in advocating for the rights of these marginalized groups, ensuring their inclusion in decision-making processes and protecting their cultural heritage.

Furthermore, environmental challenges and sustainability have gained importance in Latin America. Human rights monitoring and accountability mechanisms have been instrumental in holding governments and corporations accountable for environmental abuses, promoting sustainable practices, and protecting the rights of communities affected by environmental degradation.

International organizations have played a significant role in shaping Latin American policies. Through their engagement and support, these organizations have helped strengthen human rights monitoring and accountability mechanisms, providing technical assistance, and facilitating dialogue between governments and civil society.

Lastly, the influence of globalization on Latin American economies and cultures cannot be overlooked. Human rights monitoring and accountability mechanisms have played a crucial role in ensuring that globalization does not lead to the violation of human rights or exacerbate inequalities. These mechanisms have been vital in protecting workers' rights, combating child labor, and promoting fair trade practices.

In conclusion, human rights monitoring and accountability mechanisms have been instrumental in shaping the political, social, and economic changes in Latin America. They have contributed to political transitions, democratization processes, and the recognition of marginalized groups' rights. By holding governments and other actors accountable, these mechanisms have promoted justice, democracy, and respect for human rights in the region.

Chapter 11: The Influence of Globalization on Latin American Economies and Cultures

Globalization and Economic Integration

In recent decades, Latin America has witnessed profound changes in its political, social, and economic landscape. One of the most significant factors driving these transformations is the process of globalization and economic integration. This subchapter aims to provide a comprehensive analysis of the impact of globalization on Latin American economies and cultures, and its implications for diplomats and politicians.

Globalization has brought both opportunities and challenges to Latin America. On the one hand, it has opened up new markets and investment opportunities, leading to increased foreign direct investment and economic growth. The integration of Latin American economies into global value chains has enabled them to tap into global markets and access advanced technologies. This has boosted exports and facilitated the diversification of economies, reducing reliance on traditional commodities.

However, globalization has also exposed Latin American economies to increased competition and vulnerability to external shocks. Neoliberal economic policies, which were widely adopted in the region during the last half-century, have emphasized trade liberalization, deregulation, and privatization. While these policies have contributed to economic growth, they have also led to increased inequality and social disparities. The benefits of globalization have often been concentrated in the hands of a few, exacerbating poverty and marginalization.

Moreover, globalization has not only affected Latin American economies but also had profound cultural implications. The influence of foreign cultures, primarily from the United States, has led to the homogenization of cultural practices and the erosion of traditional values. This has sparked debates about cultural identity and the need to preserve local customs and traditions.

In the face of these challenges, Latin American governments have sought to strike a balance between embracing globalization and protecting national interests. Regional integration initiatives, such as the Union of South American Nations (UNASUR) and the Pacific Alliance, have aimed to promote economic cooperation and strengthen the region's bargaining power in the global arena.

Diplomats and politicians play a crucial role in shaping the response to globalization and economic integration. They must navigate the complexities of international trade negotiations, advocate for inclusive and sustainable development, and ensure that the benefits of globalization are equitably distributed. Furthermore, they must address the social and environmental challenges brought about by globalization, such as the protection of indigenous rights, gender equality, and environmental sustainability.

In conclusion, globalization and economic integration have had a profound impact on Latin America. While it has opened up new opportunities for economic growth and development, it has also brought about significant challenges. Diplomats and politicians must navigate these complexities and ensure that the benefits of globalization are shared by all, while safeguarding cultural diversity and promoting sustainable and inclusive development.

Foreign direct investment and export-oriented industries

Foreign direct investment (FDI) has played a crucial role in the development of export-oriented industries in Latin America over the last half century. This subchapter will explore the relationship between FDI and these industries, and the impact it has had on the political, social, and economic changes in the region.

FDI has been vital for Latin American countries seeking to diversify their economies and reduce their dependency on traditional sectors such as agriculture and mining. By attracting multinational corporations (MNCs) to invest in export-oriented industries, these countries have been able to tap into global markets and benefit from increased trade and economic growth.

One of the key reasons why Latin America has been attractive to foreign investors is its vast natural resources and low labor costs. MNCs have been drawn to industries such as manufacturing, textiles, and electronics, where they can take advantage of the region's competitive advantages. This has led to the creation of jobs, increased productivity, and improved living standards for many Latin Americans.

However, the relationship between FDI and export-oriented industries has not been without its challenges. Critics argue that MNCs often extract resources without considering the long-term environmental and social consequences. They point to instances where local communities have been displaced, and ecosystems have been damaged due to unsustainable practices.

In recent years, there has been a growing awareness of the need for sustainable development in Latin America. Governments and civil society organizations are increasingly pushing for responsible investment practices that prioritize social and environmental sustainability. This has led to the emergence of initiatives such as the United Nations Global Compact, which encourages businesses to adopt socially responsible policies.

Furthermore, the rise of populism in Latin America has also had an impact on FDI and export-oriented industries. Some populist leaders have pursued policies that prioritize nationalization and protectionism, which can discourage foreign investors. This has created uncertainty and hindered the growth of these industries in some countries.

In conclusion, foreign direct investment has been instrumental in the development of export-oriented industries in Latin America. It has brought economic growth, job creation, and technological advancements to the region. However, it is essential for policymakers to strike a balance between attracting foreign investment and ensuring sustainable development. By adopting responsible investment practices and addressing social and environmental concerns, Latin American countries can maximize the benefits of FDI while minimizing its negative impacts.

Cultural homogenization and cultural preservation efforts

In the last half century, Latin America has undergone significant political, social, and economic changes. These transformations have not only shaped the region's development but have also had a profound impact on its diverse cultural fabric. One of the key challenges faced by Latin American countries today is the tension between cultural homogenization and cultural preservation efforts.

As Latin America opened up to the forces of globalization, there has been an increasing influence of Western culture and values on the region. This phenomenon of cultural homogenization has been driven by factors such as the spread of mass media, the rise of consumerism, and the dominance of English as the global language. While these developments have brought about certain benefits, they have also raised concerns about the erosion of traditional cultural practices and identities.

Recognizing the importance of cultural diversity and the need to preserve local traditions, Latin American countries have embarked on various initiatives to safeguard their heritage. Efforts have been made to promote indigenous languages, preserve archaeological sites, and protect traditional art forms. Additionally, cultural festivals and events have been organized to celebrate and showcase the rich diversity of Latin American cultures.

However, cultural preservation efforts face several challenges. Economic pressures, urbanization, and migration have led to the marginalization of indigenous communities, threatening their cultural practices and knowledge systems. Furthermore, the influence of globalization and the dominance of Western culture can be seen in various aspects of daily life, from clothing and music to food and entertainment. This raises questions about the authenticity and sustainability of cultural preservation efforts in the face of globalization.

To address these challenges, policymakers, diplomats, and politicians must recognize the importance of cultural diversity as a source of strength and resilience for Latin America. Efforts should be made to integrate cultural preservation into national development plans, ensuring that traditional knowledge and practices are valued and protected. Furthermore, international cooperation and collaboration can play a crucial role in supporting cultural preservation initiatives, providing funding, expertise, and technical assistance.

In conclusion, the tension between cultural homogenization and cultural preservation efforts is a complex issue that Latin America must navigate in the context of its political, social, and economic changes. While globalization poses challenges to cultural diversity, concerted efforts are required to ensure the preservation and promotion of Latin America's rich cultural heritage. By recognizing the importance of cultural diversity and integrating cultural preservation into national development plans, Latin America can forge a path to progress that is both inclusive and sustainable.